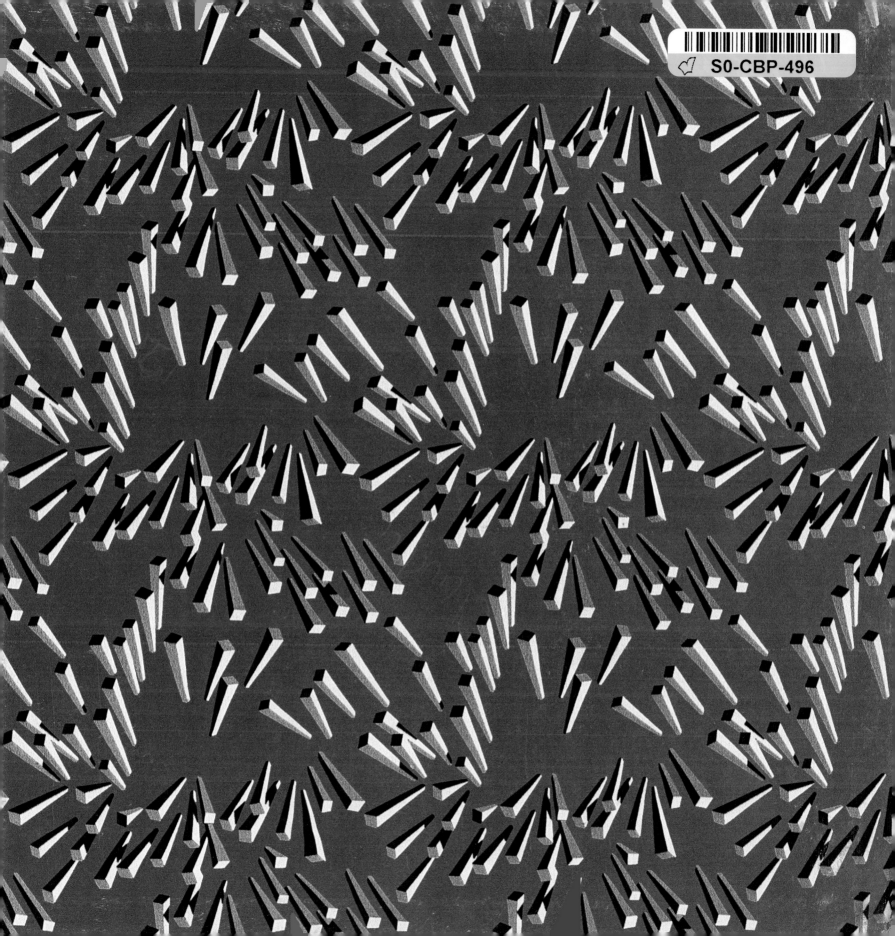

American Modern

HARRY N. ABRAMS, INC.,

PUBLISHERS

IN ASSOCIATION   WITH THE

                                            AMERICAN FEDERATION

                                            OF ARTS

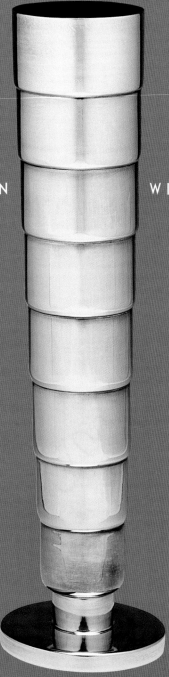

American Modern

1925–1940 • Design for a New Age

By J. Stewart Johnson

For the AFA:
Publication Coordinator: Michaelyn Mitchell

For Harry N. Abrams, Inc.:
Project Manager: Margaret Kaplan
Editor: Elisa Urbanelli
Designer: Robert McKee

Library of Congress Cataloging-in-Publication Data
Johnson, J. Stewart.
    American modern, 1925–1940: design for a new age
       p. cm.
    Includes bibliographical references and index.
    ISBN 0–8109–4208–9 (Abrams: cloth) / ISBN 1–885444–12–5
    (AFA: pbk.)
       1. Decorative arts—United States—History—20th century—Exhibitions.
    2. Decorative arts—New York (State)—New York—Exhibitions.
    3. Metropolitan Museum of Art—Exhibitions. I. Title.
    NK1404 .J65 2000
    745'.0973'0747471—dc21   99–53254

Color photography and rephotography of archival images by Joe Coscia, Jr.,
Photography Studio, The Metropolitan Museum of Art

Harry N. Abrams, Inc.
100 Fifth Avenue
New York, N.Y. 10011
www.abramsbooks.com

American Federation of Arts
41 East 65th Street
New York, N.Y. 10021
www.afaweb.org

This catalogue has been published in conjunction with "American
Modern, 1925–1940: Design for a New Age," an exhibition
organized by The Metropolitan Museum of Art and the American
Federation of Arts. Support has been provided by the National
Patrons of the AFA.

The American Federation of Arts is a nonprofit art museum service
organization that provides traveling art exhibitions and educational,
professional, and technical support programs developed in collabo-
ration with the museum community. Through these programs,
the AFA seeks to strengthen the ability of museums to enrich the
public's experience and understanding of art.

EXHIBITION ITINERARY TO DATE

The Metropolitan Museum of Art
New York, New York
May 16, 2000–January 7, 2001

Mint Museum of Craft + Design
Charlotte, North Carolina
May 3–July 28, 2002

Page 1: Walter von Nessen. *Table Lamp*, 1928 (page 60)
Page 2: Kem Weber. *"Today" Vase*, 1927 (page 50)
Page 6: Edward J. Steichen. *"Americana Print: Moth Balls and Sugar"
    Textile*, 1926 (page 72)
Page 16, Fig. 10: Emile-Jacques Ruhlmann. *Cabinet.* The
    Metropolitan Museum of Art, Purchase, Edward C. Moore Jr.
    Gift, 1925 (25.231.1)
Page 28, Fig. 19: John Storrs. *Forms in Space, Number 1.* The
    Metropolitan Museum of Art, Francis Lathrop Fund, 1967
    (67.238)

Contents

Acknowledgments

American Modern, 1925–1940: Design for a New Age continues an ongoing cooperation between The Metropolitan Museum of Art and the American Federation of Arts for traveling exhibitions designed to share the museum's rich and varied resources with other museums around the country. This, the first traveling exhibition of selections from the Modern Design and Architecture Collection, has been made possible by combining the Metropolitan's holdings with those of the John C. Waddell Collection. A recent and very important promised gift to the museum, the John C. Waddell Collection is exceptional in its thorough representation of the work of the first generation of modernist designers living and working in America. The Metropolitan has had a long history of involvement in the espousal of modern design, most notably in presenting landmark exhibitions of American industrial design in 1929, 1934, and 1940 and by acquiring important examples over the years. The John C. Waddell Collection greatly enriches the museum's holdings in this area, increasing both their depth and breadth. We are delighted that these works and the curatorial concept that unifies them are being given national exposure.

In addition to our gratitude for the generosity of Mr. Waddell, we express deep appreciation to William S. Lieberman, Jacques and Natasha Gelman Chairman of the Department of Modern Art, for his ongoing support; and to J. Stewart Johnson, consultant for modern design and architecture, for his selection of the works and for his authorship of the catalogue.

We wish to thank Joe Coscia, Jr., in the Metropolitan's Photograph Studio, for his exceptional catalogue photography. For their contributions to both the exhibition and this publication, we also wish to thank the following staff members in the Metropolitan's Department of Modern Art: Jane Adlin, curatorial assistant; Jared Goss, senior research assistant; and former interns and fellows in the department: Aric Chen, Masha Chlenova, Paul Franklin, and Melissa Kerr. We would like to acknowledge as well the contributions of Barbara Bridgers in the Photograph Studio, Aileen Chuk in the Office of the Registrar, and Marceline McKee from the Loans Office.

At Harry N. Abrams, the copublisher of this book, our appreciation goes to Margaret Kaplan, senior vice president and executive editor; Elisa Urbanelli, senior editor; and Robert McKee, designer, for their patience and dedication.

We also thank those members of the AFA staff whose efforts have been important to the realization of this project: Thomas Padon, director of exhibitions; Susan Hapgood, curator of exhibitions; Michaelyn Mitchell, head of publications; Brian Boucher, interim head of education; Lisbeth Mark, director of communications; Mary Grace Knorr, registrar; Beth Huseman, publications assistant; Jennifer Jankauskas, exhibitions assistant; and Stephanie Ruggiero, communications assistant. We gratefully acknowledge the support of the National Patrons of the AFA.

Philippe de Montebello
Director, The Metropolitan Museum of Art

Serena Rattazzi
Director, American Federation of Arts

Design for a New Age

I. Awakening

As a major ally of France in World War I, the United States was offered a prime site in the great 1925 Paris Exposition des Arts Décoratifs et Industriels Modernes. There was, however, one condition. The world's fairs of the past had been showcases providing national exhibitors opportunities to display their most impressive wares. The emphasis was on the skill of each nation's craftsmen and—more important, as one of the chief aims of these fairs was the promotion of trade—the prodigious capabilities of the new machinery developed in the Industrial Revolution to mass-produce goods for sale. Objects might be executed in any style, and the great majority of those exhibited were in fact based on historic models. Now, however, the French imposed a new set of ground rules. In setting the conditions for participation in the 1925 fair, the organizers stipulated:

> Works admitted to the Exposition must show new inspiration and real originality. They must be executed and presented by artists, artisans, and manufacturers who have created models and by editors who represent the modern decorative and industrial arts. Reproductions, imitations, and counterfeits of ancient styles will be strictly prohibited.[1]

The operative word was *modern*. Faced with this demand for modernity, Herbert Hoover, then United States Secretary of Commerce, canvassed educators, businessmen, and prominent figures in the American art establishment and on the basis of their advice declined the French invitation. His advisors' judgment: there was no modern design in America.

As Charles R. Richards—a leading educator who would head the American commission that Hoover subsequently sent to Paris to report on the exposition and its implications for American industry—wrote: "A review

Fig. 1. Catalogue cover of the 1926 touring exhibition of objects culled from the 1925 Paris exposition. Classical maidens, antelope, and baskets of flowers were favorite Art Deco motifs.

A Selected Collection of Objects from the International Exposition of Modern Decorative & Industrial Art

PARIS

1925

Organized and Exhibited by
The American Association of Museums

of the arts for the past century shows little but a varied kaleidoscope of the older motives, barren for the most part of new ideas and lacking wholly in coordination of effort toward distinct modern styles." He went on to explain, and to some extent excuse, this judgment:

> In America we assumed our place as a nation practically at the time of the industrial revolution. We had no artistic tradition except those of the mother countries where the old order was shortly to turn into the new. Furthermore, the material needs of life absorbed all the energies of our people. As we expanded and became prosperous the genius of leadership was absorbed in the development of our natural resources, the expansion of our railroads, the opening up of our mines, the felling of our forests, the building of factories and the organization of our industries. Naturally, under such conditions, we looked to the old world for our artistic leadership.[2]

Richards wrote this in 1922. The book in which it appeared was not published until 1929, and by then the attitude toward design had already begun to change in America. It would continue to do so over the next decade, and at an increasing pace. By the time the United States entered World War II, a pioneer group of American designers, abandoning historical ornament, employing new materials and technologies, and working closely with industry, had developed a new style that was at once modern and recognizably American. At first much of their work reflected the catalytic influence of the Paris fair. Quickly, however, they moved away from the elegance of the French Art Deco style, first toward the clean, uncluttered lines and pure geometric forms espoused by the German Bauhaus and then toward the less mechanistic approach of Scandinavian functionalism. Still, though the American designers were aware of and influenced by European design currents—and indeed many of them had emigrated from Europe—as their work evolved, it took on a distinct character of its own.

The emphasis of the French Art Deco style was on luxury. Its products were typically characterized by costly materials and fine workmanship. Its designers primarily aimed their wares at a small, affluent clientele. In contrast, American designers sought to capture the broadest possible market, substituting machine production for handcraftsmanship. And although the Americans came to assimilate much of the design aesthetic of the Bauhaus, they were not motivated by the social idealism that lay behind it. Their aim was not so much to bring good design within reach of the masses—a goal the Germans were ultimately unable to achieve—as to produce fresh, affordable products that would appeal to a rapidly expanding middle class. In seeking to create objects appropriate to life in twentieth-century America, and in response to the specific social and economic conditions that prevailed here, they forged a new style that to a great extent would transform the American domestic landscape.

When, in fact, the Paris fair opened, it became apparent that the modern spirit the French had demanded of the participants was not so revolutionary after all. The great majority of French displays bore a reassuring resemblance to familiar objects from the past, specifically those produced from the end of the eighteenth

Fig. 2. Pavilion of the Paris department store Grand Magasins du Louvre at the 1925 Exposition des Arts Décoratifs et Industriels Modernes. Studium Louvre was the store's design component.

through the early nineteenth centuries. Unexpected, sometimes violent, colors lent many of the exhibits an air of originality, as did occasional jagged decorative patterns derived from Cubism; but the forms to which they were applied, from buildings to small decorative objects, more often than not were based on a pared-down Neoclassicism. The pavilions erected by major French commercial interests—manufacturers such as Lalique and Sèvres, the design studios run by the large Parisian department stores, and the leading *ensembliers* Emile-Jacques Ruhlmann and Süe et Mare, who might be thought of as the *hauts couturiers* of the decorative arts— were all symmetrically planned, and most incorporated conventional motifs in their decoration (figs. 2, 3). Pilasters, dancing nymphs, and elegant animals in low relief (antelope, deer, and borzois were especially favored); cornucopias and baskets of flowers; swags of drapery; and representations of fountains in wrought iron, ceramic, or glass—all these abounded. The exhibits within the pavilions, often arranged as room settings, tended to be formal; and the great majority of furniture was formal as well. Grand dining rooms were featured (fig. 4), and the decorative schemes of many of the salons were centered on massive commodes, frequently inlaid with rare woods, ivory, or mother-of-pearl. The majesty of commodes and bedsteads was in some cases further emphasized by placing them on low platforms (fig. 5). Seating furniture was upholstered in tapestry or

Fig. 3. The Ruhlmann pavilion at the 1925 Exposition des Arts Décoratifs et Industriels Modernes. Rigidly symmetrical and decorated with relief panels of dancing maidens, it was conceived as the villa of an art collector.

silk. Elaborate crystal chandeliers and wall sconces lit the rooms, the walls of which were hung with silk or richly patterned paper. After the devastation of the war, which had destroyed much of the industry devoted to the decorative arts, shutting down workshops and in many cases claiming the lives of craftsmen, the organizers of the fair obviously saw the 1925 exposition as their great chance to reestablish the hegemony of France in the *industries de luxe*.

There was another side to the fair. Amid the welter of essentially conservative pavilions, there was a bare handful of structures designed in a truly modern spirit. Konstantine Melnikov's Russian pavilion featured walls painted a symbolic red, large areas of glass, and an exterior staircase that sliced diagonally through the building, dividing it into two sharply angled triangles (fig. 6). Robert Mallet-Stevens's information and tourist pavilion was surmounted by an uncompromisingly geometric clock tower (fig. 7); and the sculptors Jan and Joel Martel provided four "Cubist" trees, the limbs of which were cantilevered slabs of reinforced concrete, for one of the little gardens that punctuated the fairgrounds (fig. 8). They were all ridiculed by press and public alike.

The most notorious intruder in the exposition's otherwise vast homogeneous sea of Art Deco was Le Corbusier's Pavillon de l'Esprit Nouveau (fig. 9). A mock-up of a model duplex apartment unit, it had an asymmetrical plan, stark window walls, and a covered living terrace (which had to be built around an existing tree). Before it stood an abstract sculpture of a female nude by Jacques Lipchitz. Le Corbusier's pronouncement in his book *Vers une Architecture* (1922) that "a house is a machine for living in" had made him the whipping boy of those who opposed

Fig. 4. Dining room of the Lalique pavilion at the 1925 Paris exposition.

Fig. 5. Bedroom designed by André Groult. The furniture was enriched
with sunburst patterns of sharkskin and ivory.

modernism, and when he requested space on which to erect his display, the organizers of the fair managed to find an obscure corner into which it might be tucked unobtrusively. The commissioners hid the building from view with a high fence during its construction, and it was not certain until the opening day that they would permit him to remove the hoarding.

Striking and ultimately significant as these modernist exhibits were, they were the exceptions. The overwhelming message of the Exposition des Art Décoratifs et Industriels Modernes was one of chic, elegance, and ostentation. Ironically, the balance might have shifted if Germany had been permitted to participate. Modern design had made much stronger inroads in Germany than in France. Walter Gropius's brilliant new building complex for the Bauhaus was completed in Dessau in 1925, as was Marcel Breuer's first tubular-steel furniture; had the Bauhaus masters and students exhibited in Paris in 1925—as they finally managed to do in 1930—the course of French decorative art might have been changed and the so-called Art Deco style, which lingered in France through the 1930s, been brought to a speedier end. This, however, was not to be. Anti-German sentiment was so strong in France in the aftermath of World War I that an invitation to Germany, though rancorously debated in the French press while the fair was being planned, was finally deemed to be impossible.

The exposition was a huge success. Attendance topped sixteen million. Hordes of American tourists traveled to Paris to see it, among them a number of the men and women who in the next decade would lead the American design movement. Although they went to marvel, however, few of the American visitors seem to have returned home persuaded that what they saw on display had much relevance to them. Helen Appleton Read, one of the more perceptive American critics, warned her readers:

The exotic and the ultra are perhaps overstressed in the furniture and displays of interior decoration. It must be remembered, however, that this is an exposition and a French one at that, and that it is only natural for the Frenchman with his love

Fig. 6. Konstantine Melnikov's Russian pavilion at
the 1925 Paris exposition.

of display to dress up and upholster his ideas. Also the dictum "to be different and modern" brought with it the inevitable corollary of the freakish and the faddish. This is especially so in the case of the manufacturers, who without a spark of real creative genius have nevertheless gone about designing chairs and tables in what they believed to be the modern spirit. It has been carried to an ad absurdum degree as, for example, sharkskin furniture, macabre bedroom schemes in violet black and bluish purples, jade and jeweled salons de bain, furniture representing negro sculpture, monkeyskin bedspreads and glass walls. The American manufacturer looking for something modern French to incorporate in his new line can hardly be blamed if he does not feel right in recommending to the little bride, bent on furnishing her apartment in the newest thing, backgrounds which would awaken dreams of Baudelaire or Guy de Maupassant.[3]

Fig. 7. Tourist pavilion by Robert Mallet-Stevens at the 1925 Paris exposition. Its clock tower provided a startling contrast to the Grand Palais and the Italian pavilion, between which it was sandwiched.

Still, despite the critics' barbs and a general perception that what was being served up in Paris was too precious to be adaptable to the American lifestyle, there was a disquieting feeling that the Europeans were on to something and that we were being left behind. This was particularly galling, as it challenged the popular American self-perception that of all nations the United States was the most innovative, the most up-to-the-minute. In fact, the American public was considerably less open to new ideas than it chose to admit. Change could be threatening, particularly change originating overseas. Paradoxically, Americans were at once deferential before European culture and essentially xenophobic.

There were those who refused to believe that American conservatism was immutable. These optimists were convinced that sooner or later the country would have to come to terms with the twentieth century. Without subscribing to any particular aesthetic, they nonetheless recognized that there was an invigorating new spirit abroad, one that spoke to the new century and looked toward the future rather than the past; and they were convinced that the American public must be won over to it. They believed that if objects designed in the modern spirit were readily available, they would find their way into American homes and offices. But before that could happen, the general public had to be made to find them desirable so that manufacturers would be convinced that it was worth their while to invest in new designs. It was a classic chicken–egg dilemma: without objects there could be no demand; without demand there would be no objects. Charles Richards tried to persuade the manufacturers that the development of newly designed products was a good business proposition:

At present we pay a heavy toll to Europe for art products and designs. It is not only desirable to save this outlay but to gain the increased value for our goods that higher artistic standards will bring. The United States has practically but one market for the products of its art industries. Paris has the whole world as its market. In the future the expansion of our trade must take into account not only the production of goods which are required to satisfy material needs, but which may command a world market because of their artistic value.[4]

Fig. 8. The "Cubist" trees by Jan and Joel Martel at the 1925 Paris exposition.

Abstract arguments, however, were not enough to convince the manufacturers to risk capital on new designs. What the reformers needed was to find a way to create a demand to which the manufacturers would respond.

Fig. 9. Le Corbusier's Pavillon de l'Esprit Nouveau at the 1925 Paris exposition.

Among the most influential of Charles Richards's allies were Richard F. Bach and Joseph Breck, who from their positions in New York's Metropolitan Museum of Art were able to proselytize for the new style. Bach had been hired in 1918 to act as a liaison between the museum and manufacturers, designers, dealers, and craftsmen in an attempt to raise the standard of American industrial products. The museum had presented a modest display of objects produced by American manufacturers in 1917, and this became the first of a series of "annual" exhibitions of American industrial design that Bach devised together with Joseph Breck, the curator of decorative arts and assistant director of the museum.[5] Initially, these exhibitions were restricted to objects whose design had been inspired by the study of masterworks on view in the galleries of the museum. It was obviously an approach that encouraged copying rather than innovation. Before long, however, the stultifying effect of this policy became apparent. Breck was traveling abroad and purchasing for the museum decorative-arts objects designed in the latest style (fig. 10). By 1923 he could write:

> If the decorative arts in Europe are speedily outgrowing the period of tutelage characterized by the copy and the pastiche, this country has contributed little as yet to the evolution of a new style. The dependence on the past, which characterizes so much of our applied art today, would be disheartening were it not, as we confidently believe, merely a stage in the evolution of taste—a period of assimilation which will be followed in due time by one of original expression. In matters of art we learn from the past; but, apprentice days over, we must make our own contribution to the living tradition of art.[6]

Still, it was not until 1926 that any real change could be seen in the museum's policy. That year it presented two strikingly different exhibitions devoted to contemporary design. The tenth annual design show, titled "Exhibition of Current Manufactures Designed and Made in the United States," put on display yet another familiar array of tired copies and, in some cases, bizarre pastiches of objects from the past (fig. 11). In the same year, however, the museum also played host to a major traveling exhibition of objects culled from the Paris Exposition des Arts Décoratifs et Industriels Modernes (figs. 1, 12). This exhibition, the brainchild of Charles Richards, provided the first opportunity most Americans had to see for themselves what all the fuss over modern design was about.[7] It opened in Boston and after its New York stop at the Metropolitan went on to Cleveland, Chicago, Detroit, St. Louis, Minneapolis, Pittsburgh, and Philadelphia, attracting large crowds at all venues.

The 1926 traveling exhibition of Parisian masterworks set off a remarkable sequence of ambitious shows, initially clustered in New York but soon spreading to other large cities around the country, which were intended to whip up enthusiasm for the new design. These were not presented by museums but by department stores. They were not overtly commercial—in some cases none of the objects were for sale—but frankly pedantic; every effort was made to emphasize their seriousness. Museum presidents and directors, critics, and socialites were recruited for sponsoring committees; well-printed catalogues, some containing critical

Fig. 10. Cabinet by Emile-Jacques Ruhlmann, purchased in Paris by Joseph Breck in 1925 for The Metropolitan Museum of Art. The combination of traditional form, prominent stylized decoration, costly materials (amboyna, kingwood, and ivory), and fine workmanship characterized the best of French Art Deco.

Fig. 11. Carved and painted desk and bookcase, exhibited in The Metropolitan Museum of Art's 1926 "Exhibition of Current Manufactures Designed and Made in the United States."

essays, were issued. At first, the great majority of objects on display had to be imported, and this had the effect of prolonging the impression held by many Americans that *modern* and *French* were synonymous; but 1927 saw another exhibition assembled in New York that attempted to contradict this assumption.

Titled "Machine-Age Exposition" and organized by Jane Heap of *The Little Review*, it was held in an office space on New York's Fifty-seventh Street and ran for two weeks in May. As with most of the department-store exhibitions, it boasted an "Honorary Committee" of notables (including the Metropolitan Museum's ubiquitous Richard Bach, who seems to have lent his name and support to virtually every manifestation of progressive thought about design at the time) and an unusually impressive "Artists Committee," among the members of

which were Alexander Archipenko, Charles Demuth, Marcel Duchamp, Hugh Ferriss, Louis Lozowick, André Lurçat, Elie Nadelman, Man Ray, and Charles Sheeler. The cover of its illustrated catalogue was designed by Fernand Léger (fig. 13), and the contents of the exhibition were gathered from the United States, Austria, Belgium, France, Germany, Poland, and Russia. Herbert Lippman, reviewing it in *The Arts*, described the installation:

> The setting . . . itself had significant form. This was the unpainted white plaster finish of walls, columns, beams, girders and floor slabs of an unpartitioned office floor of a common type of building erected for commercial renting. . . . Radio sets, valves, gears, propellers, metal cupboards, ventilators, aeroplanes, diving apparatus, rifles and machine guns, slicing machines, harvesting

Fig. 12. Objects by Armand Albert Rateau, as they were exhibited at The Metropolitan Museum of Art in 1926.

implements, scales, gas manufacture, piano frames, motor car designs and electric light bulbs were among the exhibits. These stood about like the pieces at a sculpture exhibition, on pedestals of a sort, numbered and catalogued.[8]

This was a far cry from the bandbox treatment afforded the Parisian imports by the department stores. Here the hero was not the decorator but the engineer. In celebrating the "dynamic beauty" of machines and machine-made utilitarian objects, it anticipated the Museum of Modern Art's "Machine Art" exhibition of 1934—perhaps better remembered because by 1934 public taste had evolved to the point where a machine aesthetic no longer could be easily dismissed.

The following year another highly significant exhibition opened in a Fifty-seventh Street office building. This was the American Designers' Gallery (fig. 14). Herman Rosse, its president, later described its inception:

Fig. 13. Fernand Léger's cover for the catalogue of the 1927 "Machine-Age Exposition" in New York.

> During 1927, Mr. Edgar A. Levy asked me to give him some artistic advice. He wanted, he said, to do something to promote art and asked me what form such aid should take. I suggested to him that he form a group of American designers interested in industrial and applied art and invite them to hold an exhibition in some centrally located gallery in comparison with the exhibits held from time to time in the large department stores of European designs in the same field. He liked the idea and asked me to invite such a group of designers and to engage a manager to carry the business end of the undertaking.[9]

Rosse described the roster of exhibitors as being "like lifting a page from an Almanac de Gotha of American design of that period." Thirty-six exhibitors were listed in the catalogue, including Alexander Archipenko, George Biddle, Donald Deskey, Hunt Diederich, Paul T. Frankl, Maurice Heaton, Pola and Wolfgang Hoffmann, Raymond Hood, Ely Jacques Kahn, Ilonka Karasz, William Lescaze, Peter Müller-Munk, Henry Varnum Poor, Ruth Reeves, Herman Rosse, Edward Steichen, Joseph Urban, and William Zorach. Here, for the first time, was a group of American designers banding together to display their own works and proclaiming their Americanism. The installation comprised ten room settings, each by a different designer, surrounding a central court containing cases of objects and displays of architectural work. The most admired ensemble was Donald Deskey's "Man's Smoking Room" (fig. 15), which Adolph Glassgold, an astute critic, said took "top honors . . . by the beauty of its design, astonishing ingenuity, and absolute comfort."[10] He commended it as "one of the outstanding contributions to the modern style" and pointed out that though it was "composed exclusively of standard industrial materials," the designer had "employed our machine-made products without the slightest trace of mechanicalness." Deskey's room had an aluminum ceiling (the one element of which Glassgold did not approve). Otherwise, he described it as follows:

> Small tables of black Vitrolite and metal braces stand upon a dark linoleum floor on which lies a tan rug of Deskey's design. The light tan pigskin chairs and sofa match a desk of tulip wood edged with aluminum. Tan and brown cork walls are recessed for a mirrored bar, a large window, and two bookshelves, above which, in excised aluminum tubes, are contained the lights.[11]

The use of industrial materials such as cork, linoleum, metal, and Vitrolite would become an essential ingredient of the emerging American modern style, as, ultimately, would the attempt to divorce machine production from a machine aesthetic.

Among the other rooms commented on by Glassgold were a bedroom by Winold Reiss ("no startling departures in design or arrangement"), Ilonka Karasz's nursery ("one of the gayest, jolliest and most practical rooms ever designed for a child"), Joseph Urban's boudoir ("over-elegant"), and the ceramicist Henry Varnum Poor's bathroom ("an exciting adventure in color"). Perhaps the most original was Herman Rosse's dining room (fig. 16 and page 86). Glassgold termed it a tour de force, and indeed it was. Ceiling, walls, furniture, even the plates and bowls on the table were all made of metal. The ceiling and walls were spray-painted a deep blue; and the effect, in the designer's words, was "reminiscent in its precise technical finish of motor cars and yachts."[12] The same blue was carried through in the corduroy upholstery of the polished metal chairs, the velvet curtains, and the linoleum floor. The walls were bent into a series of curves and opened to reveal shallow shelving, unpainted and polished to a mirror finish. The entire ensemble glistened. All in all, it was too much for

Fig. 14. Ilonka Karasz's cover for the 1928 American Designers' Gallery exhibition.

Fig. 15. Donald Deskey's "Man's Smoking Room" in the American Designers' Gallery exhibition. (Donald Deskey Collection, Cooper-Hewitt National Design Museum, Smithsonian Institution, Art Resource/NY)

Fig. 16. Corner of Herman Rosse's metal dining room in the
American Designers' Gallery exhibition.

Glassgold, who concluded that it was "an interesting experiment but an unsuccessful one."[13] In its urbanity and extreme sophistication, however, it presaged much that would follow in the next decade.

Virtually all of the designers who showed their work in the American Designers' Gallery were also members of the American Union of Decorative Artists and Craftsmen, known by its acronym, AUDAC. Formed in 1928, this broad-based group included industrial designers, decorators, architects, photographers, and craftsmen. During its short life, its members organized two exhibitions and published a book. The first exhibition, entitled simply "Home Show," was installed in New York's Grand Central Palace in 1930; it featured five modern room settings in a handsome overall installation designed by the architect Frederick Kiesler, as well as smaller displays of objects designed by members (fig. 17). This was followed in 1931 by a larger exhibition, "Modern Industrial and Decorative Art," at the Brooklyn Museum. The group is remembered today, however, less for its exhibitions than for the ambitious book it produced illustrating a cross section of executed work by its members. It was published in 1930, between the first and second shows, under the title *Modern American Design* and quickly reprinted as the *Annual of American Design 1931 (see page 69)*. Sadly, the new title was overly optimistic; there were to be no more books nor any more AUDAC exhibitions.

Fig. 17. Frederick Kiesler's installation for the 1930 "Home Show" of the American Union of Decorative Artists and Craftsmen (AUDAC) in New York's Grand Central Palace.

II. Reactions

How did all these efforts to sell the new design go down with the audience they were supposed to influence? From time to time, magazines and newspapers took note of the exhibitions in museums and department stores, usually with illustrated news stories and occasionally with critical essays. Adolph Glassgold, writing in *Creative Art,* devoted numerous articles to developments in design and architecture as seen in New York City. But perhaps the most sustained and revealing look at the public's response to the new design can be obtained by reviewing the editorials printed in *Good Furniture Magazine.* As a trade journal, it focused on home furnishings rather than attempting to report on the entire field of industrial design; still, its writers were obviously eager to keep the manufacturers, designers, and decorators who were its readers abreast of significant design trends. In June 1927, it made its first assessment of the prospects of the public's acceptance of the new style:

> The first signs of modernistic influence from France, Austria, Germany and Britain appeared a year ago. The summer markets of 1927 will show a further progression of this influence but in a conservative form. An out-and-out application of European modernistic theories in American furniture seems out of the question. American taste is too conservative to tempt our furniture manufacturers to discard historic precedent in favor of the unknown trail of the modernistic. All European attempts so far made to create furniture strictly of the present with no allegiance to his-

toric precedent, involve effects possible only by costly labor processes that do not lend themselves to quantity production.[14]

Native conservatism and the imperative need of manufacturers to produce goods that would appeal to a mass market, both factors that would largely shape the development of the new design in America, were already recognized here. This view was reinforced two months later, when the magazine cautioned that "it is yet too early to predict what sort of reception the American public will accord modernist art; that will depend largely on the form it takes and whether American methods of quantity production can be successfully applied to the new style trend."[15]

By October the magazine had changed its stance. It was no longer simply reporting on the new design, but was espousing it, if only tentatively:

> American manufacturers are by no means bold adventurers as far as art moderne is concerned. Those who are manufacturing furniture of this type are few. Yet modernist furniture is salable, and those few firms which make it declare that it sells readily. That more manufacturers have not taken up the modernist style can be accounted for, no doubt, by the fact that they have a steady demand for their own traditional styles, and deviation from established routine would mean a considerable interruption to an already successful manufacturing policy.[16]

It should be noted that in 1927 the terms *Art Moderne, modernist,* and *modernistic* were interchangeable. Before long, *modernistic* would take on a pejorative coloring, but in 1927 the whole idea of a modern design (as opposed to traditional) was so new that distinctions could not be made readily between what is now considered to be Art Deco and modernist design. In fact, few Americans had seen any examples of what we today would term *modernism*—that is, the work being produced in the Bauhaus or by designers such as Le Corbusier or Gerrit Rietveld—save the rare illustrations they may have come upon in foreign architectural journals.

By January 1928, *Good Furniture* had become an open advocate for the new design. Wanamaker's department store in New York had put together a collection, which they named "Venturus," of the "work of present-day French masters, augmented by that of numerous Americans whose creations are directly in the spirit of French modernism." The impetus that led to the creation of "Venturus" was the success of the design studios that the major Parisian department stores had set up to offer their customers a range of specially designed objects in the latest style. Au Bon Marché had "Pomone"; Au Printemps, "Primavera"; Grands Magasins du Louvre, "Studium Louvre"; and Galeries Lafayette, "La Maîtrise." Now Wanamaker's followed their lead with "Venturus." As was typical of most of the American department-store exhibitions promoting the new style, nothing on view was price-marked or to be sold; but, as the magazine pointed out:

Some of the material is commercially produced, and it is an interesting fact that bulky orders have been booked among a wide variety of objects. It is equally true that others who have ventured into the modern field cannot supply the demand for modern fitments. This is certainly a straw which shows which way the wind is blowing, in the large cities at least where live most of the folks who are able to gratify the whims of fashion in home furnishings.[17]

The same issue devoted considerable space to the "Art in Trade" exhibition at Macy's:

One of the first gestures toward modernism which really seems to mean anything in its relation to home furnishing of today has recently been made through the furniture department and decorating staff of R.H. Macy & Co., Inc. of New York, where modern merchandise has actually been installed as part of the furniture selling activities, and is being offered commercially. Hitherto, adventures into the modern, as they concern New York, have been made by those whose work appeals to a clientele prepared to pay high prices. Macy's has frankly commercialized this modern art, but based upon the soundest of foundations—consumers' demand.

The three rooms now on display at Macy's were all made after designs which Macy's decided were both modern and American enough for home approval. The prices of the original furniture are listed with a schedule of Macy's prices for its reproduction. Some of the copies of this French furniture are shown with the originals. They are excellent—in fact, identical in detail, and yet are marketed at prices which are much less than the French originals, of course.

One misses the freakish and bizarre from the Macy scheme of things. Practical, livable, comfortable rooms, done in the modern manner for modern people, offer suggestions for the fitting of the apartment or house of modern dimensions. . . . And it is not just an exhibition. Copies of every piece shown are available. In fact, the exhibition rooms were not installed until Macy's was ready to take orders (made in America, of course) for the furniture shown and the selling has eclipsed the fondest expectations. Although manufacturers seem to see little in the modern vogue, consumers eagerly snap up everything that is available. The demand is unmistakable, but its volume may, of course, not be sufficient to encourage commercial manufacturers. It does exist, though, and it seems reasonable to think that volume will develop as soon as it is possible for these demands to be fulfilled. Everybody who has a stick of modern furniture is selling it, and cannot fill the demand. Macy's recognized this trend of public taste and is prepared to profit by it.[18]

There are a number of things worth noting here. Although some of the pieces of furniture were frank knockoffs of French originals, the copies were "American enough for home approval"; that is, they avoided "the freakish and bizarre"—shades of Helen Appleton Read's criticism of the 1925 Paris exposition!—and instead were "practical, livable, comfortable." These are quintessential American virtues and are attributes that in time would come to characterize American modern design. The editorial also sounded a note of caution. Despite its ringing endorsement of modern design ("Everybody who has a stick of modern furniture is selling it"), the battle had not been won. The public may have been buying it; the manufacturers were not, at least not yet.

September 1928 saw the magazine heralding Art Moderne on the one hand as "the outstanding design trend in furniture" and on the other sounding less certain of its future.

> The furniture and textile manufacturers have been watching the new-fangled designs from Europe and American shops, waiting to see whether the American public would show enough interest to warrant taking the innovation seriously as a manufacturing proposition. The manufacturers, except in isolated instances, are not yet satisfied that it is wise for them to go into the new venture to any great extent, although the public has already shown interest most gratifying to the pioneering retailers. The summer wholesale markets seem to have increased considerably the manufacturer's suspicion that his aloofness from the modernistic was probably a mistake and that he can safely embark on the new design slant.[19]

It was beginning to look like a false spring. *Good Furniture* was hedging its bets as it went on to predict that "the design trend away from the traditional will be conservative. Radical departures will be seen but, for the most part, the retail trade will frown upon them as freaks and buy the conservative." In other words: be new, but not too new. With such equivocating advice it is easy to understand the caution of American manufacturers.

An editorial in the April 1929 issue of the magazine compared the position of designers in Europe and America, pointing out that "industrial art in Europe as a career has long been made attractive" and that "European designers, duly inspired by training and by subsequent recognition, have been developing a brilliant technique in industrial art." In contrast, in the United States,

> it was generally thought, in the furniture field, that the design of old "period" types would not have qualified our actual furniture designers to perform in the highly modern manner of the new European styles—nor were there any furniture designers so known by name that their names would have had any significance in the new trend of design. Architects, painters, stage designers and advertising artists were called upon to show America (and incidentally the world) what we could do. Considering their state of complete unpreparedness, it is not at all remarkable that their work seems to lack the finish, decision, and manner of corresponding work by European designers. The remarkable thing is that their work is as good as it is.[20]

This was faint praise indeed, and the editor's condescension toward native-born American designers was compounded when he added:

> When Eugene Schoen,[21] Joseph Urban, Paul Frankl, Lucien Bernhard, Winold Reiss, and Pola
> Hoffmann appear in . . . showings of American designers, it should be remembered that, by years
> of training, practice, and experience, this group is "American" only in the matter of citizenship.
> Actually these are European designers. We see in their work a degree of certainty of finish and of
> technique which it will take most of our designers years to develop.[22]

To this roster of immigrant designers the writer could have added Walter von Nessen, Kem Weber, Peter Müller-Munk, Wolfgang Hoffmann, Frederick Kiesler, Ilonka Karasz, Herman Rosse, William Lescaze, Eliel Saarinen—the list goes on. Still, by 1929 a number of designers born in America were working alongside them and were creating objects of comparable quality. Donald Deskey, Norman Bel Geddes, Russel Wright, Gilbert Rohde, Ely Jacques Kahn, and Walter Dorwin Teague, to name only a few, had entered the field and, in the next decade, would rival the transplanted Europeans. If in time the Americans acquired some of the polish of what *Good Furniture* saw as their European betters, the Europeans (most of whom had come from Germany or Austria and brought with them design concepts closer to the stripped-down functionalism that was increasingly prevalent in northern Europe than to the more decorative conceits fashionable in France) seem to have been influenced by the Americans, their work becoming more genial and expansive, less austere.

The magazine's preoccupation with European versus American design was further explored in the August 1929 issue, with the prediction that

> both French and German furniture and interior decoration—in the modern manner—will go a
> certain distance in this country and then come to an abrupt end. Unless along with it, the design-
> ers are to give us a new heaven and earth, or an entirely Europeanized point of view, there is a
> time, not too far distant, when a group of American designers, soundly trained and keen visioned,
> must take up the challenge of the modern manner and do something real and vital with it, and
> something that is neither imported nor copied.

This call for a new American design might seem encouraging if it were not followed by the suggestion that it might be a good idea to reserve judgment for a while on the whole subject of the modern manner in interior decoration, for,

> it is quite possible, for instance, that the modern designers will develop only a new set of clichés,
> as obvious as those of the style Louis XV, or any other period—and there would be an ironic

humor in this. Let us not mistake hysteria for progress or egotism for art. The millennium may be close at hand, but it has not, in this year of grace 1929, quite yet arrived.[23]

A month later, an editorial titled "Still a Question" cast further doubt on the staying power of the modern style by suggesting that it might well share the fate of Art Nouveau and Mission, both of which turned out to be passing fashions and were now discarded, and warning its readers that "once they were modern."[24]

By March 1930 the magazine's editorial titled "Where Are Our Moderns?" took the dimmest possible view of the state of American design. It began by looking back to

that memorable March of 1927 when first New York, and then the country at large, was galvanized into amazement and enthusiasm by the exhibition of modern French furniture and decorative art at Lord & Taylor. Everything, people were sure then, would be "modern" or,—if one wanted to be more fancy, "moderne." A new era of taste had dawned. The old would go very quickly into the discard. Most of the predictions of that time, now three years ago, have not, somehow, come off.

It then went on to ask:

Today, where are our moderns? Who are they? Who in any conspicuous, significant way is translating the accomplished European idea of modern decoration into an American idiom? Three years is not a long time, to be sure, and yet it is long enough to show some progress, some direction, some evidence that we are getting somewhere with the new ideas. At the moment of writing there seem to be not even any exhibitions of modern interiors from which we could gauge our progress as creative designers. . . . Have we, in fact, no inventive or resourceful designers? It begins to appear so.[25]

Good Furniture and Decoration (as the magazine now called itself), in its April 1930 editorial, neatly tapped the final nail into the coffin it had recently begun to fashion for the American modern movement. Marveling at "the amazing public attendance and . . . gratifying sales that marked the recent Antiques Exposition held at Grand Central Palace in New York," it reminded its readers that "it is generally recognized that every manufacturer of furniture or decorative accessories realizes the definite advantage to his business that comes from a popular appreciation of fine antiques" and that "the most practical significance of antiques is their stimulating effect on the appreciation and desire for worthy reproductions and adaptations in the homes of the country." That said, it went on to consider the "extraordinary popularity of the Antiques Exposition . . . as a commentary on the status of the *'moderne'* (or whatever may be one's favorite name for it)." Modern was now both italicized and put within quotation marks and, if that were not enough, was dismissed with "or whatever may be one's favorite name for it." The writer summed up:

> We are forced to the conclusion that, in spite of various things seen in print from time to time, the *moderne* isn't the 100 per cent sweep, even here in New York, that its adherents claim for it. In other words, there must be something wrong with the often-heard statement that "everything's modern now." It appears that everything *isn't* modern.[26]

What went wrong? In three short years the magazine had gone from interest, to enthusiasm, to outright advocacy, to retreat and, finally, rejection of a modern American aesthetic. It may be that the furniture manufacturers to whom it addressed its editorials by 1930 had decided that modernism was merely a fad and unworthy of investment. *Good Furniture* was, after all, servicing the trade and presumably less interested in crusading than in reporting on and reflecting the concerns and attitudes of its subscribers. It had tried to gain widespread acceptance for the new movement, but these last editorials strongly suggest that it believed it had failed.

In 1928, Adolph Glassgold, writing in *The Arts,* noted the first faltering attempts to delineate a modern American style:

> America is beginning to take a keen interest in the modern movement among our own designers and if today, the interest appears unwarranted by the material presented, we may be assured from all indications, that a vigorous and worthy form is evolving that shall be neither imitation French nor diminutive skyscrapers.[27]

"Imitation French" never caught on; however, there was more to be said for skyscrapers. They were potent symbols of modernity, and they were uniquely American. In the 1920s and 1930s, the ultimate attribute of success was a penthouse apartment in Manhattan. If the bungalow was the typical housing in the period leading up to World War I and the tract house that of the years following World War II, it was the urban apartment that ruled in the interwar years. Then the cities acted as magnets. Paul Frankl, whose reputation was largely built on his designs for "skyscraper" furniture (fig. 18 and pages 52, 53), caught the excitement skyscrapers generated when he noted that "modernity expresses itself in the energy of the vertical thrust of towering buildings that push themselves through the crumbling red husks of the city of the past."[28] The imagery of skyscrapers combined with the slashing lines and sharp planes associated with Cubism caught the public imagination almost at once. The painters Georgia O'Keeffe, Bernard Boutet de Monvel, and Charles Sheeler; the sculptor John Storrs (fig. 19); and photographers such as Berenice Abbott and Margaret Bourke-White all attempted to capture the beauty of the great towers rising in New York. Skyscrapers inspired textiles, lamps, cocktail shakers (the most evocative symbol of the period's quest for sophistication), and furniture.

Fig. 18. "Skyscraper" bookcase by Paul T. Frankl.

Frankl's designs for furniture suggesting the staggered setbacks of sky-scrapers were much admired, but all too often attempts to bring the giant constructions rising in Manhattan down to a domestic scale resulted in clumsy caricatures. They were described by one writer as "the grotes-queries of lightning flashes, of geometric nightmares, of form climbing onto form."[29] Even at its best, the skyscraper phase of modern design was too extreme to attract a broad market for anything beyond the occasional accessory.

Once the eccentricities of skyscraper-inspired forms were eliminated, the next stage of American modern design could emerge. This was a mod-ernism closely allied with that which was increasingly gaining acceptance abroad. Frankl set down its basic characteristics as "(1) simplicity; (2) plain surfaces; (3) unbroken lines; (4) accentuation of structural necessity; (5) dramatization of the intrinsic beauty of materials; (6) the elimination of meaningless and distracting motives of the Past."[30] He might have added one other particularly American ingredient to this formula: streamlining. He had recognized the fascination with speed and the potency of streamlining as a symbol when, having remarked "the energy of the vertical thrust of towering buildings," he went on to enumerate the ways in which modernity expressed itself "in the speed of high-powered motors; in rapid transportation; in the Transatlantic liners; streamline construction of motorboats, airplanes and the flights of Colonel Lindbergh; in the general stripping for action, and the unimpeded release of youthful energy in sports and now especially in the arts."[31] Designers, responding to the allure of speed, began to apply streamlining to all sorts of objects—not only to locomotives, where it made sense, but to vacuum cleaners, where it did not (figs. 20, 21). The fad for streamlining reached its peak in the mid-1930s; though it was sometimes carried to absurd lengths, the quantity and overall quality of objects it brought forth suggest an enthusiasm among the public and an increasing confidence among the designers. By the end of the decade, it would give way to a less assertive style, but streamlining remains the style that epitomizes the period.

The "dynamic beauty"[32] of machines and the lure of speed caught the imagi-nation of the age. As early as 1916, in his autobiography, Henry Adams had spec-

Fig. 19. Forms in Space, Number 1 by John Storrs.

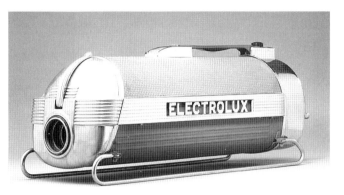

Fig. 20. Locomotive designed by Raymond Loewy for the Pennsylvania Railroad in 1936. Its smooth bullet shape, which hid the steam engine's functional elements, and the sweeping horizontal lines applied to its surface symbolized speed.

Fig. 21. Lurelle Guild's 1937 Electrolux vacuum cleaner. Although, at best, it could be dragged across the living-room floor, its streamlined design suggested the powerful thrust of a moving vehicle.

ulated on the least time it might take ocean liners in the future to make transatlantic crossings. The Italian Futurists had endeavored to capture the anarchic beauty of a machine-driven world in their paintings, poems, and architectural fantasies. In 1925, *The Little Review* went so far as to assert, in full caps, "THE MACHINE IS THE RELIGIOUS EXPRESSION OF TODAY."[33] Of course, not everyone was a believer. Aldous Huxley demurred from the enthusiasm held by many for the machine aesthetic.

> Personally, I very much dislike the aseptic, hospital style of furnishing. To dine off an operating table, to loll in a dentist's chair—this is not my ideal of domestic bliss. But I have no doubt whatever that it is destined to become (under the pressure of economic necessity and of mass suggestion through advertisement) the domestic bliss of all but a very few rich people in the future. The time, I am sure, is not far off when we shall go for our furniture to the nearest Ford or Morris agent. Le Corbusier's dream will have come true; the home will have all the appearance of a machine for living in.[34]

Still, despite the complaints of critics such as Huxley, the glamour of the machine aesthetic was undeniable and played directly into the hands of the young industrial designers attempting to create products for manufacturers in search of increased sales. William H. Baldwin concluded that "the spirit of the machine age is quantity production at a low cost per unit with rapid consumption and frequent changes in style and design."[35] The exigencies of the Great Depression of the 1930s would call forth the concept of "planned obsolescence," the aim of which, by means of the frequent restyling of products, was to make this year's consumer dissatisfied with last year's purchase.[36] But even in the prosperous twenties it was recognized that the attraction of the new could generate sales.

III. Benchmarks

Between the first and second world wars, The Metropolitan Museum of Art played a major role in fostering progressive design in America and encouraging American designers. It was not the first museum to attempt to bring an awareness of new design currents to the public; credit for that goes to the Newark Museum, where John Cotton Dana presented a landmark exhibition of modern German design as early as 1912. Nor were its design exhibitions necessarily the most innovative; in 1934, for example, the year the Metropolitan presented a sweeping survey of new domestic work by recognized designers, the Museum of Modern Art held its "Machine Art" exhibition and the Philadelphia Museum its "Design for the Machine." Although these had been preceded by *The Little Review*'s 1927 "Machine-Age" show, their sponsorship by major museums served to validate the linkage between art and the machine. The Metropolitan did not go so far. Still, the sustained effort it made in support of the new design as it evolved through the period was unique. Three of its so-called annuals—the eleventh (1929), thirteenth (1934), and fifteenth (1940)—were particularly ambitious and influential. Leading architects and designers were chosen for each and asked to design and produce entire room settings, with all their furnishings. Everything had to be new; no object on display could be taken from existing production. Looking at the rooms created for the annuals, it is possible to trace the trajectory of taste through the period.

The Metropolitan's 1929 exhibition "The Architect and the Industrial Arts" included thirteen room settings designed by nine architects. The catalogue proudly proclaimed that "not only are the objects shown of contemporary design and of American conception, but they have been designed for the specific purpose of this showing" [37] (fig. 22 and page 76). Originally scheduled to run from February 12 to March 24, the exhibition was so popular that it was extended until September 2 and was seen by more than 186,000 people. Henry Kent, the assistant secretary of the museum, explained the decision to place the exhibition in the hands of architects rather than designers by saying that so far as "effectiveness, recognition, and power" were concerned, professional designers did not exist; but "by substituting for the professional designer for the industries the designer of buildings, the architect, with his strong position in relation to the manufacturing world and his strategic position with regard to the dictation of styles to be used, [the exhibition] has been able to give illuminating exposition of what might result in the realm of design if the designer himself were to occupy a position of authority." [38] It is a statement that reveals just how tenuous the position of the industrial designer still was.

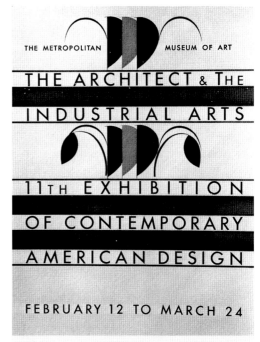

THE METROPOLITAN · MUSEUM OF ART

THE ARCHITECT & THE

INDUSTRIAL ARTS

11TH EXHIBITION

OF CONTEMPORARY

AMERICAN DESIGN

FEBRUARY 12 TO MARCH 24

Fig. 22. Poster for The Metropolitan Museum of Art's 1929 annual industrial design exhibition, designed by W. A. Dwiggins. The show was so popular it was held over until September 2.

Fig. 23. John Wellborn Root's Art Deco "Woman's Bedroom," designed for the Metropolitan Museum's 1929 exhibition "The Architect and the Industrial Arts."

John Wellborn Root's "Woman's Bedroom" is a perfect illustration of the Frenchified approach to design (fig. 23). It might almost have been lifted intact from the 1925 Paris exposition. The room's proportions were imposing. The walls were covered with velvet striated vertically in shades of gray, and the ceiling was "flesh-color and gray-rose in a pattern of arcs and right lines."[39] The three tall windows along the back wall, reaching from floor to ceiling, were hung with swagged overdraperies of printed taffeta and curtains that the architect described as being "of velvet on which transparent designs are etched—a novelty."[40] The carpet was dark rose. The large boat-shaped bed, its head- and footboards upholstered in padded blue silk, was raised on a platform in the French manner, backed by a mirror, and set within an alcove. The blue upholstery of the chaise longue matched that of the bed, and the coverlet casually thrown across it added to the room's impression of careless luxury. The sole innovative note in the ensemble was provided by the dressing table and revolving chair, which were made of pewter; but they were a far cry from the revolutionary tubular steel furniture designed by Marcel Breuer, Ludwig Mies van der Rohe, and Le Corbusier that by 1929 was being produced in Europe.[41] The top of the dressing table was engraved with a decorative pattern of swans and geese, and its kidney shape was conventional. It could have been made of wood as easily as of metal.

Fig. 24. Raymond Hood's "Business Executive's Office" for the Metropolitan Museum's 1929 exhibition.

Metal played a much larger role in the "Business Executive's Office" designed by Raymond Hood (fig. 24). Here the large L-shaped desk, the couch, swiveling chairs, chandelier, and desk lamp were all made of aluminum (thin bars rather than tubes). Charles R. Richards commented that their design represented "the first successful use of metal for this purpose" that he had seen and that they contrasted "most favorably with the metal pipe structures now being made in France and Germany."[42] The walls and ceiling were covered with Du Pont Fabrikoid. Behind the desk was a vast twenty-four-light metal-framed window hung with louvered rayon curtains woven with a pattern of chevrons. The floor was carpeted with what Richards described as a "fine rug with broken geometrical spaces."[43] The large map of the United States on the wall was hung from a rod and left unframed. If the angled lines of the furniture seem somewhat fussy to us today, still the general impression of the office is commonsensical. The dominant lines of the room were horizontal, whereas those of the Root bedroom were vertical. In every way it was more progressive—except, and it is a big exception, for the glass in the window, which took up most of the rear wall. Hood filled it with an etched design of giant conventionalized flower forms, very Art Deco and out of keeping with the furniture. It contradicts the relative restraint of the rest of the room and may have seemed to the architect to be an antidote to an otherwise unacceptable austerity. Whatever the reason, the flowery window, both stylish and pretty, worked against the otherwise sober effect of the office.

Compare Hood's office with the one designed by Raymond Loewy and Lee Simonson for the Metropolitan's 1934 annual (fig. 25). The imagined client was obviously an industrial designer. A model of a streamlined automobile was placed on a pedestal and drawings of a streamlined ship posted on the bulletin board; both were by Loewy. The entire room was sleek and streamlined. The walls and cabinets were of ivory and gray-blue Formica; all of the metal had a gunmetal finish. The corners of the room were rounded, as was the end of the long horizontal window of frosted glass. There were no curtains or blinds, and the window frame was reduced to a thin metal strip. These strips were repeated throughout the entire composition (inlaid horizontal lines encircled the walls and ran across the fronts of the low built-in cabinets, where they substituted for conventional drawer pulls). The cantilevered writing desk and drafting table extended the dominant horizontal line under the window. The floor was polished linoleum. The only movable pieces of furniture in the room were the tubular-steel chairs on either side of the desk and the tall stool at the drafting table, which were all upholstered in yellow leather. Illumination was provided by recessed spotlights set flush in the ceiling above the corner display pedestal, by built-in standing lamps that served a double function as supports for the cantilevered desk and drafting table, and by tube lights sheathed in metal flanking the cork bulletin board. The clock above the bulletin board sported a blue mirrored-glass face and ivory plastic numerals. Five years had passed since Raymond Hood produced his office design, and it was a new world.

Although the Loewy/Simonson office was the most strikingly modernist installation in the 1934 show, it did not differ radically from those of the other designers who participated in the exhibition. Eliel Saarinen, who in 1929 had shown a dining room with tall-backed chairs, inlaid cabinets, and patterned walls and carpet (fig. 26 and pages 44, 45), this time presented a radically simplified "Room for a Lady" (fig. 27). His 1929 dining room had been rigidly symmetrical, its multiplicity of patterns and vertical accents reminiscent of turn-of-the-century interiors by architects such as C. F. A. Voysey, Henry van de Velde, Frank Lloyd Wright, and Peter Behrens—and, in fact, those Saarinen himself had designed before he left Finland. The 1934 room bore no resemblance to it. The only link between 1929 and 1934 was Saarinen's inclusion of a handwoven wall hanging by his wife, Loja, in each of them. The earlier hanging fit perfectly within the busy decorative scheme; the new one struck a jarring note. This was not a place for handicraft. Apart from Loja Saarinen's hanging, the 1934 "Room for a Lady" was entirely urban and of the moment. It would have made a per-

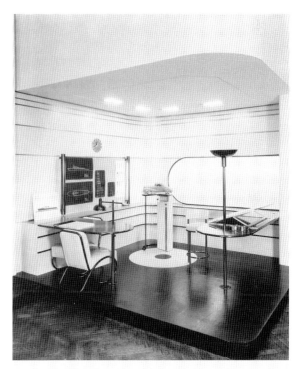

Fig. 25. Office of an industrial designer, by Raymond Loewy and Lee Simonson, in the 1934 industrial design exhibition at The Metropolitan Museum of Art.

fect set for a sophisticated Hollywood comedy of manners. The emphasis throughout was on horizontals: the furniture, almost all of which was built in, was kept low; long horizontal strips were substituted for drawer pulls on the cabinets, as they were in the Loewy/Simonson office. The color scheme was simple but dramatic. The furniture, walls, ceiling, curtains, and carpet were all white. Contrast was provided by the coral upholstery on the couch, the low circular lounge chair, and the dressing-table bench, and by the black geometric figures in the corners of the carpet and on the large pillows on the couch. The most striking single object was a large globular silvered tea urn placed on a circular table at the front of the room, near the visitor (page 106). Despite its simplicity, the "Room for a Lady" was not austere; rather, it gave a strong impression of elegance and chic. But this was not French chic. The rooms in the Metropolitan's 1934 exhibition were unmistakably American. As an editorial in *Arts and Decoration* put it:

Fig. 26. Eliel Saarinen's dining room, designed for the Metropolitan Museum's 1929 exhibition.

> You cannot look at the self-assured rooms in the Metropolitan Show, with fresh colors and synthetic materials finding natural relationship in new expression, without seeing over your shoulder the shadow of those less certain forms called "modernistic" which preceded them. These angular and steel-conscious wraiths of former exhibitions at the Museum, and of shops and window displays of yesterday, remind us that the concepts which gave us modern design have at last got out of the gawky adolescent stage.[44]

Between 1929, when it had seemed prudent to put modern design in the hands of architects rather than designers in order to assure its being taken seriously, and 1934, industrial design had reached the status of a profession. American designers, both immigrant and homegrown, had gained confidence, and with their surer approach had come public recognition. In the fiercely competitive climate of the Great Depression, manufacturers, anxious to give their products a fresh look, increasingly relied on their advice. Still, though modern design was being talked about, it had by no means been granted universal acceptance. In fact, one of its earliest champions, Charles Richards, seemed to turn against it in 1935:

> Pursued as a style, modernism becomes too often stark, eccentric, devoid of charm, alien to all tradition, and unassimilable with other expressions of design. . . . If we conceive the real basis of the

Fig. 27. Eliel Saarinen's "Room for a Lady," designed for the 1934 exhibition at The Metropolitan Museum of Art. Its simplicity was in sharp contrast to the multiplicity of patterns in his 1929 dining room.

modern movement as an emphasis rather than a style, we are freed from dogmatism and intolerance. We no longer feel the need of condemning the old because it is old, but can bend our efforts solely to produce things thoroughly adapted for the requirements of modern life. If we look at our problem in this fashion we see at once that there is as much in traditional motives, as for instance in the simpler English and American furniture of the late eighteenth century, that is well fitted to serve as a basis for modern creations, both from the standpoint of utility and charm and from the ease with which they can be adapted to the requirements of quantity production.

There is at the same time plenty of opportunity for creations making use of new materials and new forms, but here the problem is more psychological than practical. Bathroom and kitchen equipment is built to meet functional requirements and represents a striking example of successful design in this respect, as truly modern as a motor car. Living rooms, dining rooms, and bedrooms bring forth other problems. Here we need something more than mere functional adjustments to bodily needs. We need to satisfy the human spirit with grace and charm and variety. We need the familiar, and often the things dear to us by association.[45]

Charm. Chrome, white walls, black glass, and mirrors might be suitable, as one writer put it, for "the club, café, beauty salon, and small shop,"[46] or as another, "for department store windows, for millinery shop interiors, for smart uptown broker's offices, yes. For domestic interiors . . . [ellipsis in original] well, that is rather a question."[47] Much as they might fantasize about the glamourous life Fred Astaire and Ginger Rogers seemed to be sharing in their movie musicals, what most Americans wanted for themselves was something considerably more comfortable. Top hat, white tie, and tails were fine in Hollywood or on Broadway, but they were not for Main Street. And manufacturers and designers alike realized that Main Street was their market.

Fig. 28. Donald Deskey's "Sports Shack," as it was installed in the 1940 industrial design exhibition at The Metropolitan Museum of Art.

This realization became fully apparent in the last of the Metropolitan's three major industrial design shows, which was presented in 1940. It was by far the largest. More than a thousand works by 238 designers and manufacturers were shown; over the sixty-three days it ran, the attendance reached 139,261. In addition to separate displays of metals, glass, synthetic textiles, ceramics, and plastics, it featured fourteen room schemes.

Looking at these 1940 rooms, it is clear that design had undergone a sea change since 1934. The urbane sophistication that had been sought after then had given way to a much more relaxed, down-home approach. Now, Russel Wright (who had not been included in the earlier shows) presented an "Outdoor Living Room"; Walter von Nessen, a "Porch"; and architect Wallace K. Harrison (also a newcomer), the "Hall of a Country House." The most emblematic installation, perfectly catching the new spirit, was Donald Deskey's "Prefabricated Cabin Interior," which he called "Sports Shack" (fig. 28).

Set up as a hunting cabin, with rifles leaning against a wall and duck decoys mounted above the open fireplace, it suggested a casual informality that, though quintessentially American, had been missing from the earlier shows. The chairs were wood, rather than metal, and leather bands were substituted for upholstery. The back of the built-in couch could be pulled up, providing an extra bunk bed. Although innovative materials were used—the walls and ceiling were constructed of sheets of a newly developed striated plywood—the emphasis was on natural materials. Textures—the shag rug, the striated walls, the wood and leather—played a far more important role than they had previously. This was a room for Everyman, easy and comfortable, right down to the board game, pack of cigarettes, and highball on the table.

Although the "Sports Shack," along with comparable rooms in the exhibition, was unquestionably American, it owed a certain debt to the unpretentious and very livable designs that were coming out of Scandinavia at the time—especially those of the Finnish architect Alvar Aalto. His furniture had been imported since 1936 and had made a deep impression on the younger generation of American architects and designers. Aalto's work suggested a way to be modern without being doctrinaire. Architect Ralph Walker conveyed something of this approach when he commented on the exhibition:

> Perhaps today's uncertainty is wholly and intellectually due to untenable premises: that the number and the cost of articles are integral parts of the design; that new materials, such as stainless steel and plastics, are necessarily more desirable than iron, wood, or bricks; that a glass fabric is more to be sought after than the most common, everyday straw matting. Each of these materials has its place, a place not easily forced by self-consciousness. Some things will be hard and shiny, other things will continue to express the love of a craftsman for his own work. It is the intelligent use of both that gives urbanity to life.[48]

Here was a middle ground, encompassing both the precision of the machine aesthetic and the nostalgic warmth of handcraftsmanship. It had taken fifteen years for modern design in America to reach this point, but it seemed finally to have come of age.

ART DECO

The first attempts to introduce a modern style appropriate to the twentieth century into American homes were heavily dependent upon current European design. Many of the first generation of modern designers in America had been born and trained in Europe, and it is not surprising that their objects reflected these origins. Walter von Nessen's "Diplomat" coffee service (page 43), for example, resembles silver that had been produced since the beginning of the century in advanced German and Austrian studios. The predominant influence, however, was French Art Deco, which many Americans discovered at the widely publicized and much visited 1925 Paris Exposition des Arts Décoratifs et Industriels Modernes. Soon American museums and, significantly, department stores began to proselytize for the new style. Classically inspired French Art Deco motifs (fig. 1, page 9) were applied to American objects such as Sidney Waugh's "Gazelle" bowl for Steuben (page 42). Most American Art Deco designs, however, lacked the assurance of their French counterparts, as can be seen by comparing the rather timid inlaid decoration on the armoire designed for W. & J. Sloane (page 41) with the bravura ivory decoration on Ruhlmann's cabinet (fig. 10, page 16).

THE DEPARTMENT STORE

The doors open, the women surge in. Escalators slowly grind their way up and down. Columns and aisles and counters stretch in endless monotony. All day long the women come; bargains on the first floor, bargains in the basement; necessities for the kitchen and luxuries for the bath.

Services of our expert decorating staff are yours for the asking. Services of our expert fashion staff are yours for the asking.

DEPARTMENT STORE SPONSORS MODERN ART —DEPARTMENT STORE AUTHORITY ON STYLE. What altruism! Everything and anything to please the customer—if it pays.

Struggle of humanity. Sales girls on tired and aching feet make their quota for the day. Floorwalkers' faces crack in never-ending smiles of ingratiation. Figures must be made, the lash is on their backs; the new and young ones come and the old and worn-out go. Human flesh and blood is turned into profit. On with the dance, the tempo must not slacken; bigger and better stores, bigger and better figures.

Above: John Vassos. *"The Department Store,"* Illustration for Contempo *(by Ruth Vassos),* 1929

Opposite: Designer unknown. *Armoire,* 1926

Exhibited in 1926 in the fifth annual Arts in Trades Club exhibition of decorative art, The Hotel Waldorf-Astoria, New York

Above: Sidney Biehler Waugh. *"Gazelle"* Bowl, 1935

Opposite: Walter von Nessen. *"Diplomat"* Coffee Service, 1933

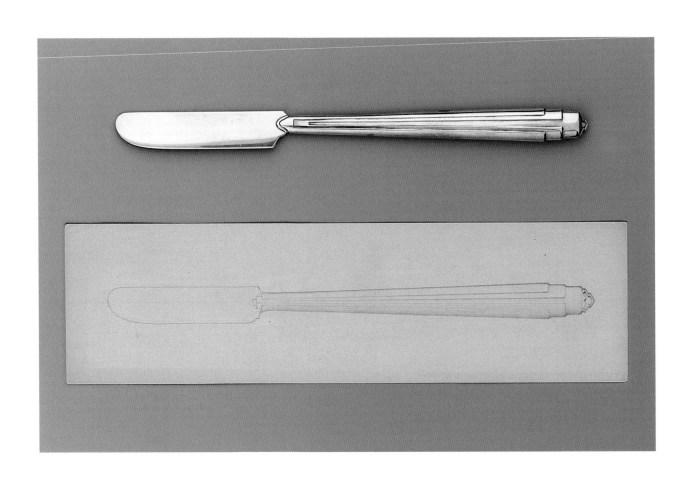

Eliel Saarinen, *Knife and Design Drawing for a Knife*, 1929

Designed for The Metropolitan Museum of Art's 1929 exhibition "The Architect and the Industrial Arts"

Eliel Saarinen. *Centerpiece*, c. 1929

A variant of this design was shown in The Metropolitan Museum of Art's

1929 exhibition "The Architect and the Industrial Arts"

SKYSCRAPERS

The jagged outline of the New York skyline was recognizable worldwide. It suggested strength, daring, a faith in the future, and a rejection of the constraints of the past. Only in the twentieth century and only in America! Artists and designers, searching for a new vocabulary with which to express the excitement and optimism of the new age, seized upon the skyscraper as a potent image and not only utilized it in paintings and sculpture (fig. 19, page 28) but applied it to everything from table lamps (page 60) to dress goods (page 47).

Paul T. Frankl wrote perceptively of the visual impact of skyscrapers (page 49) and created a successful line of "Skyscraper" furniture, the randomly stacked shapes of which were loosely based on the setbacks of the towers rising in Manhattan (fig. 18, page 28; and pages 52, 53).

Louis W. Rice. *"Skyscraper" Cocktail Shaker,* 1928

28

The horizontal line is expressive of the style of today. Here is another contribution of modern engineering to contemporary æsthetics. The horizontal expresses speed in locomotion. It denotes stability in architecture. It connotes directness, honesty and solidity. Our civilization is attuned to the horizontal line. Drawn beneath a column of figures, this line denotes finality; beneath a word, emphasis; on a wall it accentuates plane and structure. Business and thought are related to the all-significant horizontal. Our apartments are horizontal projections of the brownstone-front dwelling of other years. Streets, bridges, tunnels, viaducts—they are all monuments of our unashamed horizontalism. Industrial engineering today is bent on leveling the globe. Railroads are now cut horizontally through mountains. Steamships are bigger, steadier, endeavoring to level the sea.

51

WALKER & GILLETTE   **NEW YORK CITY**

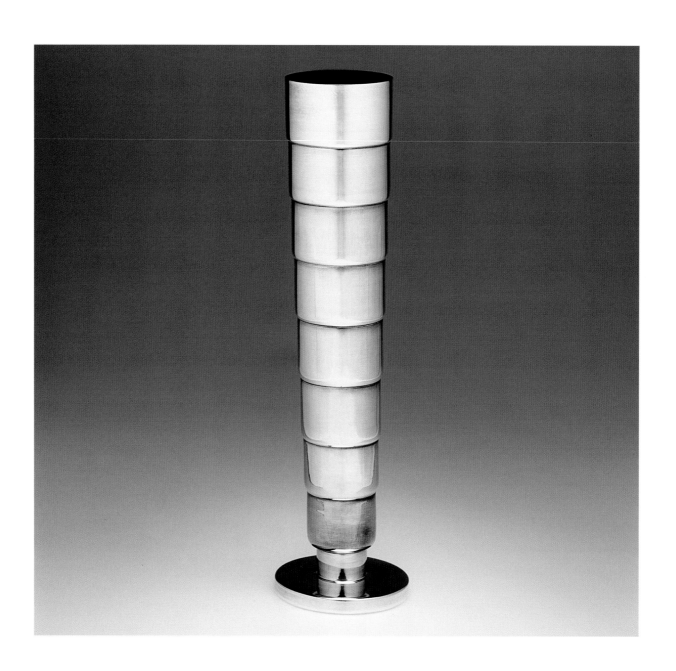

Kem Weber. *"Today" Vase*, 1927

OF THE 377 SKYSCRAPERS more than twenty stories high, which stand
in the United States in 1929, 188 rise within the narrow limits of New York City. Fifteen
of these are over five hundred feet tall; and of these fifteen, two—those illustrated on the
opposite and the succeeding page—are exactly across the street from each other.

When excavations were begun for the earlier of these—the Chanin building—
the corner of Lexington and Forty-second Street presented a fairly congested scene. True,
the Commodore Hotel across the way was a rather lowly structure,—not even thirty stories
high!—but Grand Central Station was immediately at hand, and the daily ebb and flow of
commuters made the adjacent sidewalks black.

Nevertheless, the deep excavation was made and the lofty tower raised. The
building, in itself, aroused lively interest. The architects had struck out boldly in their design;
a yet bolder lobby was designed by the owners themselves; the towering mass presents an
arresting spectacle when seen, in sharp perspective, from Forty-first and Park and,—when
seen from the viewpoint of the present drawing—the building itself bulks large against the
lurid Manhattan sky. From the uppermost floor, one gets a quite startling view across a
large section of New Jersey as well as miles of the Atlantic. Yet the flag pole was scarcely
being raised at this height, and added thousands of people pouring onto Forty-second and
Lexington, before another great excavation was begun directly across the street. . . .

THE CHANIN BUILDING
Sloan and Robertson, Architects.
Chanin Construction Company, Engineers.

· 50 ·

Paul T. Frankl. *"Skyscraper" Desk*, c. 1927

Paul T. Frankl. *"Skyscraper" Bookcase*, c. 1927

Above: Donald Deskey. *Pamphlet Cover*, 1928

Designed for the Gift and Art Shop, July 1928

Opposite: Eugene Schoen. *Etagère*, 1929

54

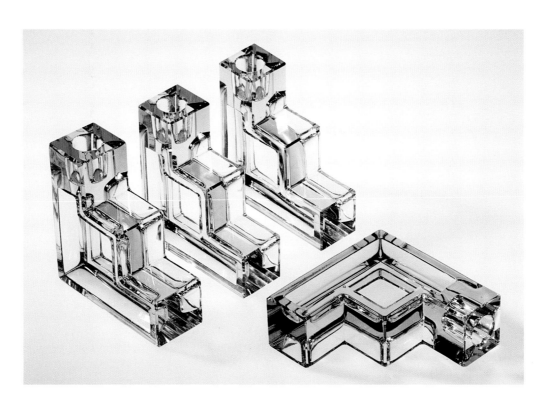

Above and opposite: Wilber L. Orme. *"Pristine Table Architecture" Series Candleholders*, 1938

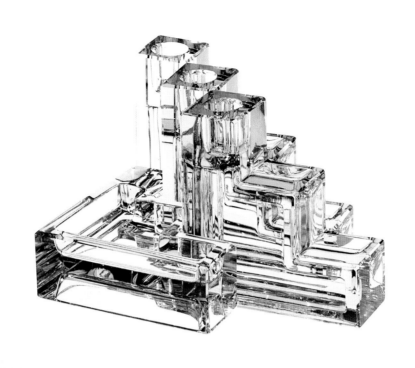

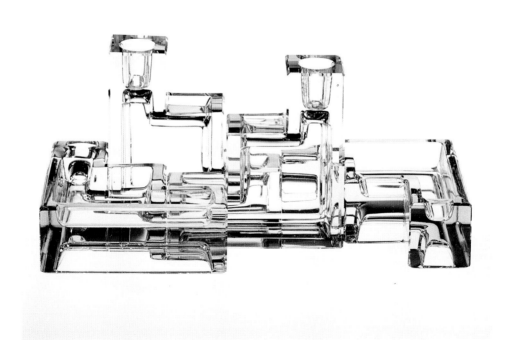

Overleaf left: Ilonka Karasz. *Coffee and Tea Service*, c.1928

Overleaf right: George Sakier. *"Lotus" Vases*, 1928

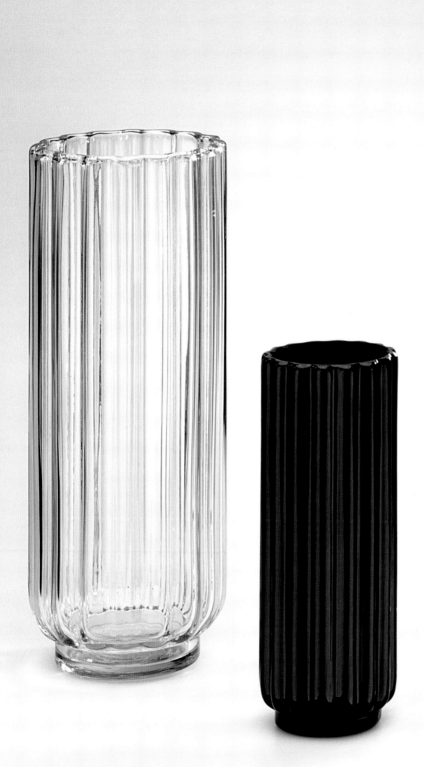

Above: Walter von Nessen. *Table Lamp*, 1928

Opposite: Walter von Nessen. *Floor Lamp*, c.1928

Lurelle Guild. *Cocktail Shaker*, c.1934

THE GRAPHIC IMAGE

For the most part, the first generation of American industrial designers eschewed conventional decoration on the objects they produced in the new style, leaving their surfaces plain. On occasion, however, they enriched these objects with geometric motifs (pages 65, 66). Their work showed the influence of avant-garde European painting and sculpture (pages 71, 122), as well as typography (pages 67, 68, 69).

One of the freshest and most imaginative uses of pattern was the "Americana Prints" collection of dress materials produced by Stehli Silks between 1925 and 1927. The company commissioned well-known artists to create designs that ranged from John Held, Jr.'s evocations of college boys and jazz bands (pages 78, 79) to a remarkable series of prints adapted from photographs by Edward Steichen of mundane objects: sugar cubes, mothballs, buttons and thread, matches and matchboxes (pages 72, 73).

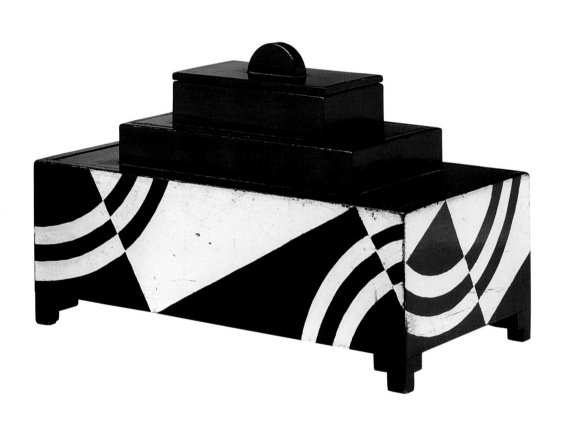

66 | Donald Deskey. *Cigarette Box,* c.1927

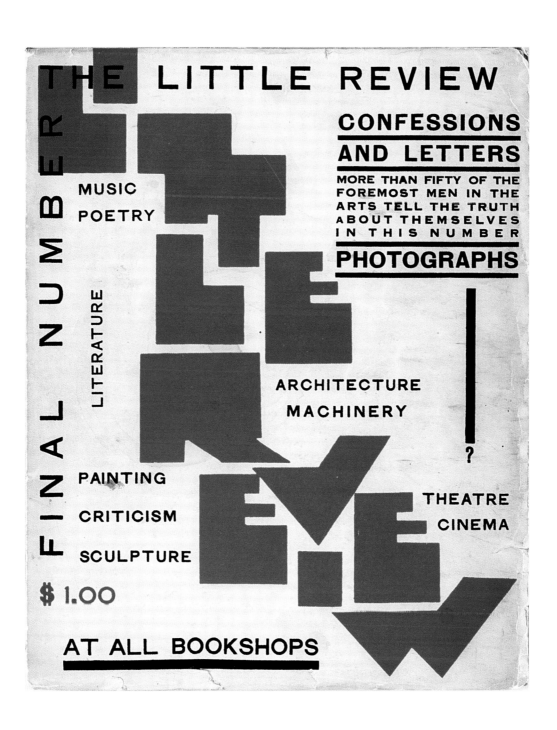

THE LITTLE REVIEW

FINAL NUMBER

CONFESSIONS
AND LETTERS
MORE THAN FIFTY OF THE
FOREMOST MEN IN THE
ARTS TELL THE TRUTH
ABOUT THEMSELVES
IN THIS NUMBER

PHOTOGRAPHS

MUSIC
POETRY

LITERATURE

ARCHITECTURE
MACHINERY

?

PAINTING

CRITICISM

SCULPTURE

THEATRE
CINEMA

$ 1.00

AT ALL BOOKSHOPS

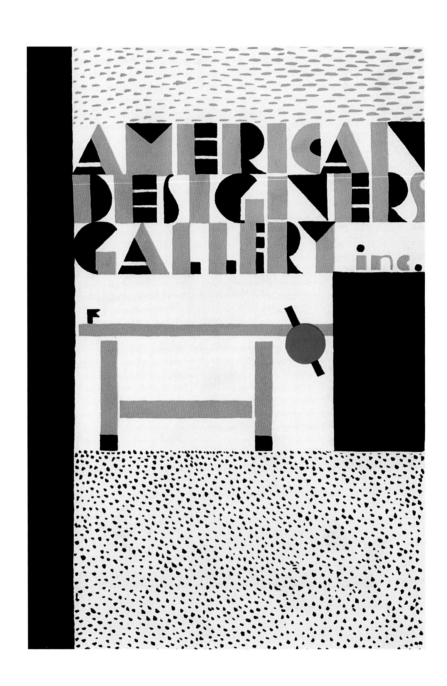

Ilonka Karasz. *Cover for Leaflet*, 1928

Designed for the 1928 American Designers' Gallery Inc. exhibition, New York

Ilonka Karasz. *Rug*, 1928

Shown in the nursery Karasz designed for the 1928 American Designers' Gallery Inc. exhibition, New York

Ruth Reeves. *"Figures with Still Life"* Wall Hanging, 1930
Designed for W. & J. Sloane, New York

71

Top left: Edward J. Steichen. "*Americana Print: Moth Balls and Sugar*" Textile, 1926

Top right: Edward J. Steichen. "*Americana Print: Sugar Lumps*" Textile, 1926

Bottom left: Edward J. Steichen. "*Americana Print: Thread*" Textile, 1927

Bottom right: Edward J. Steichen. "*Americana Print: Buttons and Thread*" Textile, 1927

72 | Opposite: Edward J. Steichen. "*Americana Print: Matches and Matchboxes*" Textile, 1926

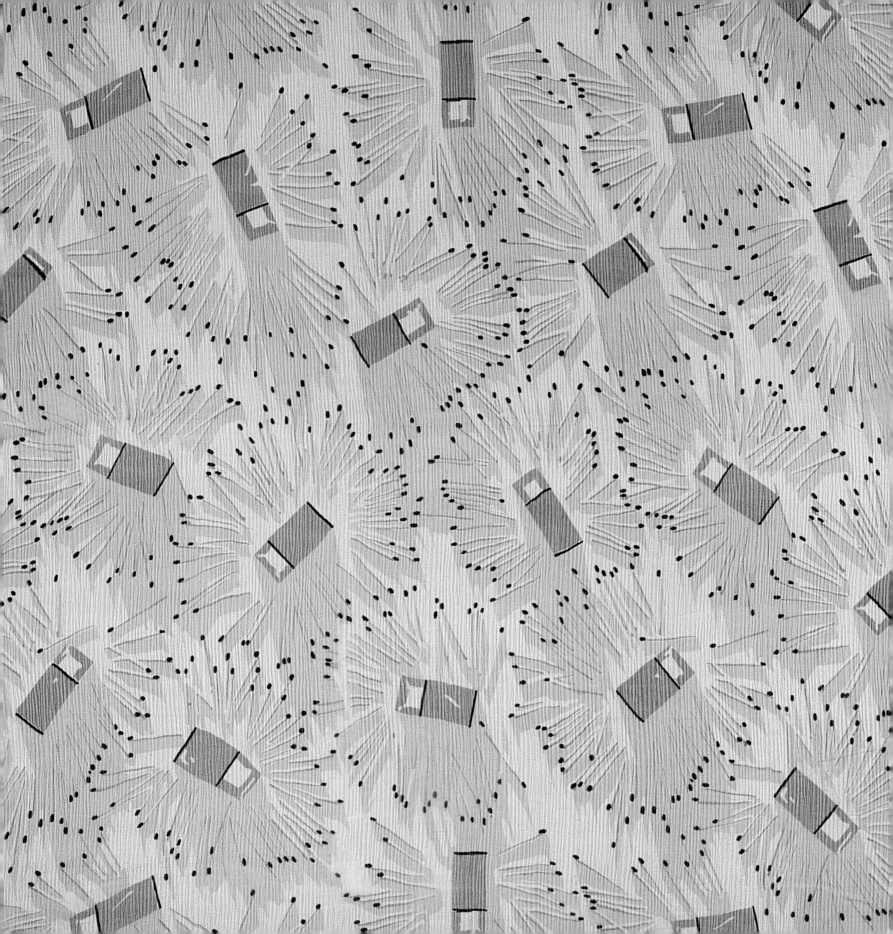

Walter Dorwin Teague. *"Flying Buttresses" Textile*, 1933

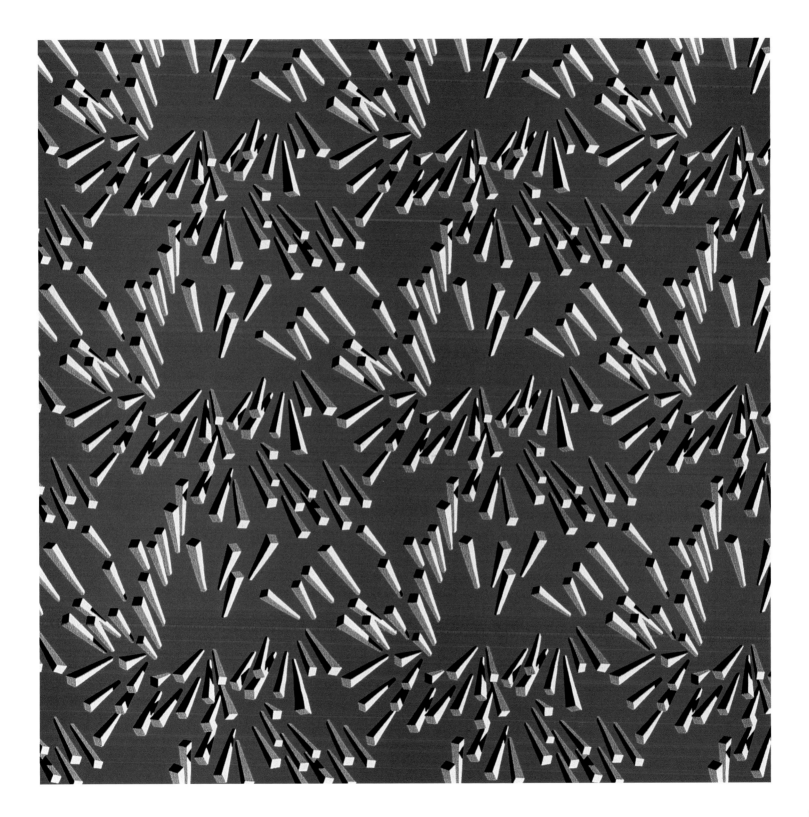

Charles B. Falls, *"Americana Print: Pegs"* Textile, 1927   75

Left: W. A. Dwiggins. *Cover for* The Architect and the Industrial Arts, 1929

Catalogue of the eleventh annual exhibition of contemporary American design held at

The Metropolitan Museum of Art, February 12–September 2, 1929

Right: W. A. Dwiggins. *Cover for* The Power of Print—and Men *(by Thomas Dreier)*, 1936

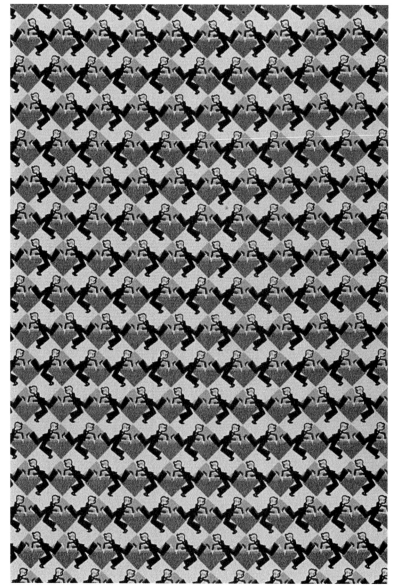

Left: John Held, Jr. *"Americana Print: 100 Per Cent"* Textile, 1926

Right: John Held, Jr. *"Americana Print: Collegiate"* Textile, 1926

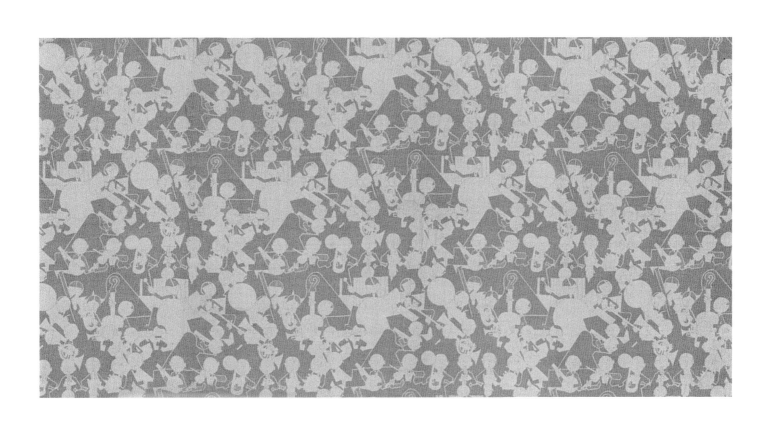

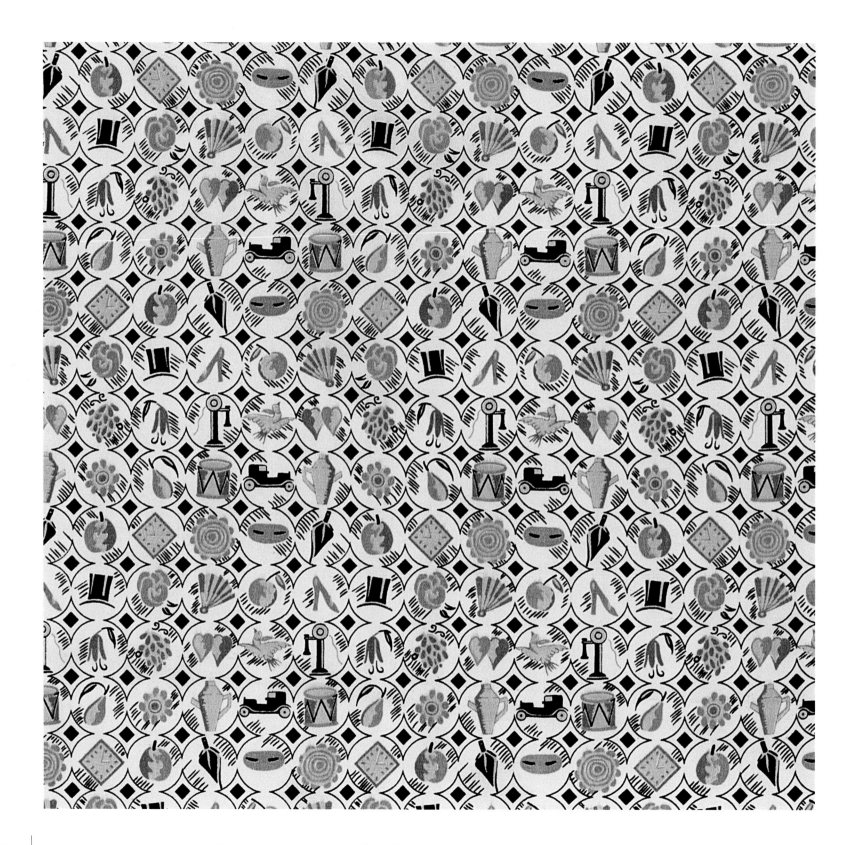

Helen Dryden. *"Americana Print: Accessories"* Textile, 1926

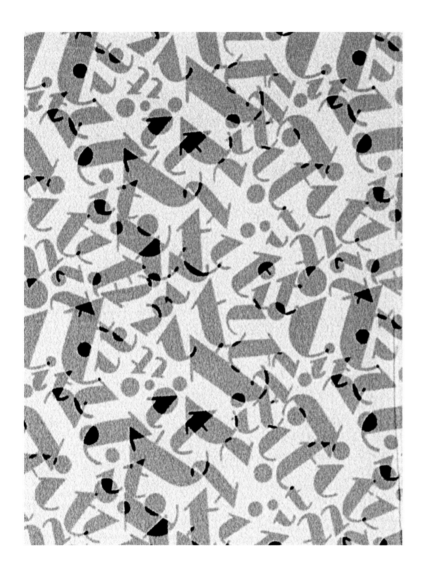

Left: Kneeland L. ("Ruzzie") Green. *"Americana Print: It" Textile*, 1927
Right: Kneeland L. ("Ruzzie") Green. *"Americana Print: Cheerio" Textile*, 1927

Ralph Barton. *"Americana Print: Gentlemen Prefer Blondes" Textile,* 1926

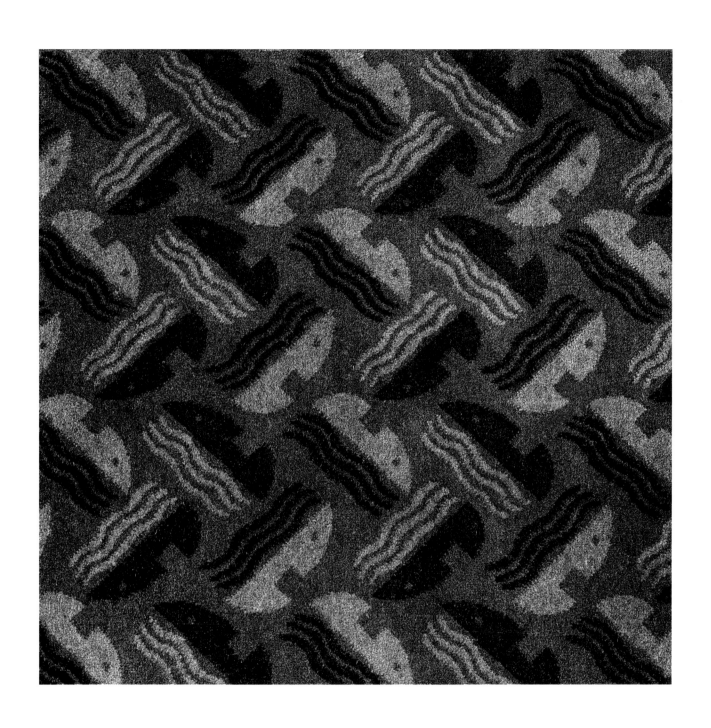

Donald Deskey. *"Singing Women" Carpet*, 1932
Designed for the main auditorium of Radio City Music Hall, New York

PENTHOUSE

The title song of Rodgers and Hart's 1936 musical comedy "On Your Toes" contained the lyric, "See the pretty penthouse / Top of the roof! / The higher up the higher rent goes. / Get that dough, don't be a goof, / Up on your toes." The penthouse atop a Manhattan skyscraper was America's ultimate symbol of success. It suggested glamour, sophistication, money. True, it might not ensure happiness—Cole Porter could have Ethel Merman sing plaintively of being "down in the depths on the ninetieth floor"—but most people, struggling to make ends meet, particularly during the Great Depression that dominated the 1930s, would have gladly traded places with her.

The penthouse represented a privileged fantasy world. Hollywood loved it, and penthouses became the favored settings for the escapist comedies and musicals that were hugely popular during the period. Their sleek furnishings—glass, lacquer, chromium—bespoke a lifestyle that was both carefree and luxurious. Interiors such as Herman Rosse's blue lacquer and chromium dining room (fig. 16, page 20; and page 86) would have been unimaginable in earlier times.

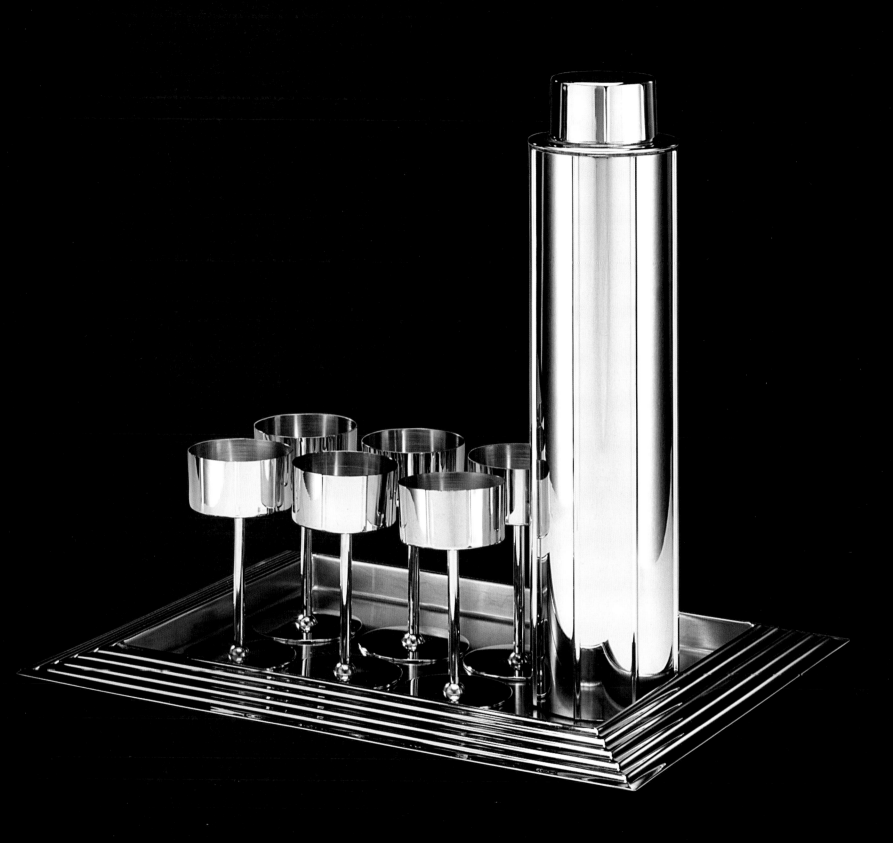

Herman Rosse. *Dining Room Accessories,* 1928

Exhibited in the dining room Rosse designed for the 1928 American Designers' Gallery Inc. exhibition

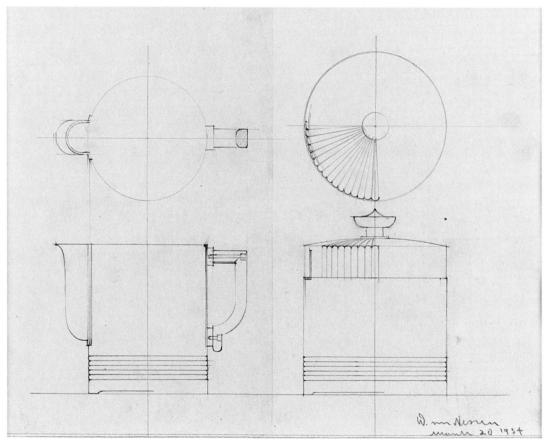

Above and opposite: Walter von Nessen. *"Continental" Coffee-Making Service and Design Drawings*, 1934

Exhibited at the 1934 exhibition *"Contemporary American Industrial Art"* at The Metropolitan Museum of Art

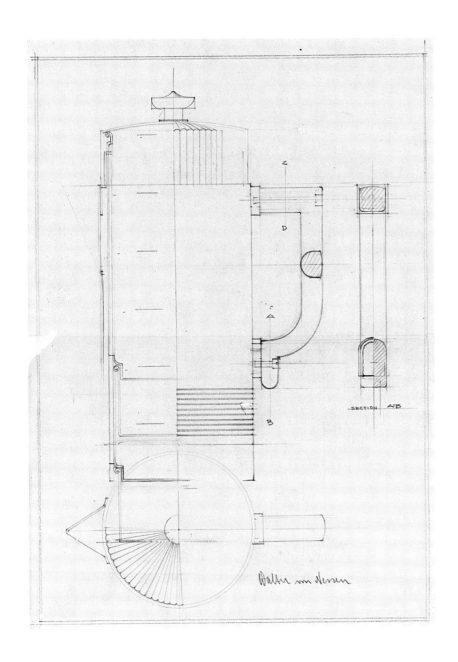

Above: Walter von Nessen. *Table*, 1930

Opposite: Donald Deskey. *Table*, c.1928

91

Above: Donald Deskey. *Table Lamp*, c. 1934

Opposite: Donald Deskey. *Console Table*, 1932

Designed for Radio City Music Hall, New York

Above: Walter Dorwin Teague. *"Bluebird" Radio,* 1934

Opposite: Designer unknown. *Low Table,* c.1937

Top: Russel Wright. *Salad-Serving Utensils*, c.1935

Bottom: Frederick Carder. *Fork and Spoon*, 1928–31

Opposite: Russel Wright. *Flatware*, c.1930

Above: Henry Dreyfuss. *Thermos Bottle and Cups*, 1937

Opposite: Norman Bel Geddes and Worthen Paxton. *"Soda King" Syphon Bottles*, 1938

Edwin W. Fuerst. *"Knickerbocker" Glassware,* 1939

Walter Dorwin Teague and Edwin W. Fuerst. *"Embassy" Stemware*, 1939

Designed for the State Dining Room, Federal Building, New York World's Fair, 1939

Above: George Sakier. *"Spool" Vase*, 1937

Opposite: Walter Dorwin Teague. *Bowl*, 1932

Overleaf left: Walter Dorwin Teague. *Vases*, 1932

Overleaf right: Lurelle Guild. *Footed Bowl*, 1934

Above: Paul Lobel. *Tea Service*, 1934
Exhibited at the 1934 exhibition "Contemporary
American Industrial Art" at The Metropolitan Museum of Art
Opposite: Eliel Saarinen. *Tea and Coffee Urn and Tray*, c. 1934
A variant of this design in silver plate was exhibited
at the 1934 exhibition "Contemporary American
Industrial Art" at The Metropolitan Museum of Art

Above: William Archibald Welden. *"Empire" Cocktail Shaker*, 1938

Opposite: Russel Wright. *Pitcher*, c. 1932

GEOMETRIES

In 1925, while the world's attention was caught by the splendid fair in Paris, an event of perhaps greater significance to design history was taking place in the small German industrial city of Dessau: the building of the new Bauhaus by Walter Gropius. Founded in 1919 in Weimar as an arts-and-crafts school, by 1925, when it moved to Dessau, the Bauhaus had as one of its chief aims the training of designers to work in partnership with industry in order to produce household objects that would be both affordable to the masses and beautiful. Bauhaus designers found beauty in pure, undecorated geometric forms—the square, triangle, and circle; the cube, cylinder, and sphere. Although the social ideals that underlaid the school ultimately went unrealized, the Bauhaus aesthetic had a wide and lasting influence on both architecture and design.

In America, avant-garde designers, responding to this stimulus, began to radically simplify objects, paring them down to basic geometric shapes that could only be drawn on paper with straight-edge and compass and only be fabricated with machinery. Handcraftsmanship seemed a thing of the past; the new age belonged to the machine. It was a brave move, but the severity of the new objects was destined to find acceptance with only a limited audience.

Russel Wright. *Spherical Vase, Planter, and Cocktail Shaker*, c.1932   111

Left: Frank G. Holmes. *Vase*, c. 1934

Right: Walter Dorwin Teague. *Vase*, c. 1934

Both shown in the 1934 "Machine Art" exhibition at the Museum of Modern Art, New York

Above: Gilbert Rohde. *Electric Clock*, c. 1933

Opposite: Walter Dorwin Teague. *Centerpiece*, 1932

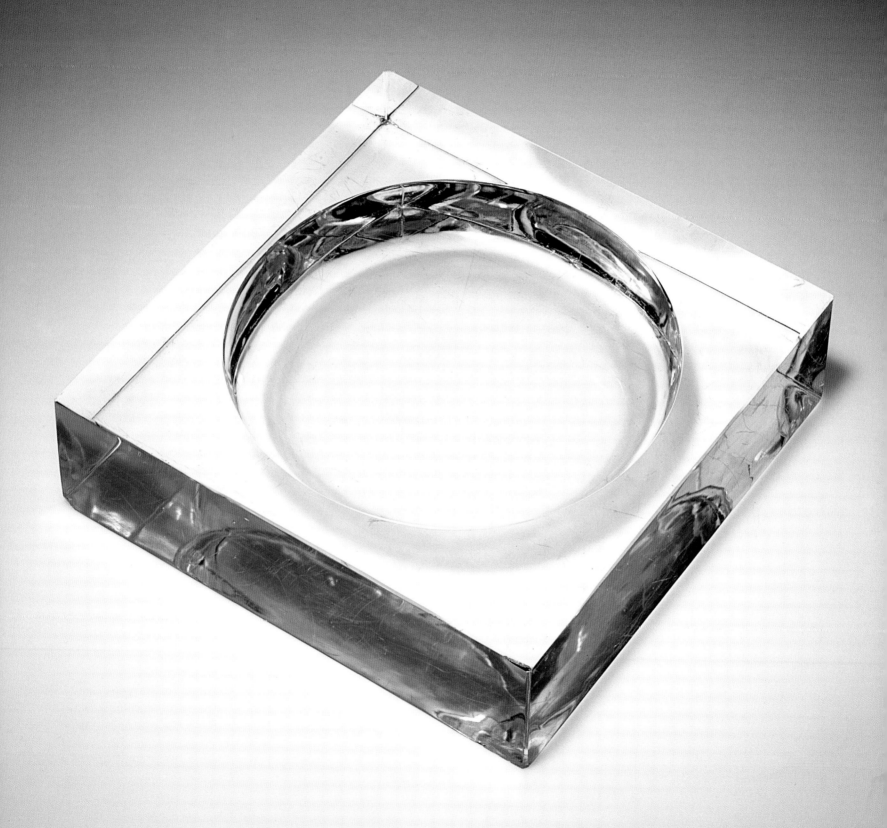

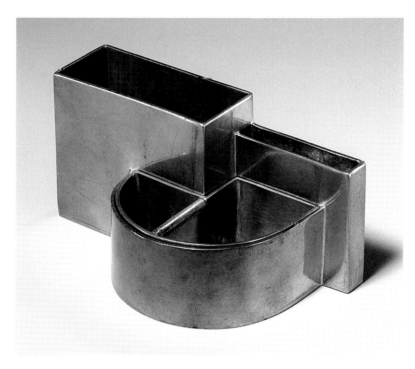

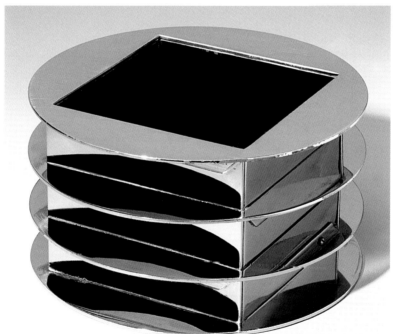

Top: Wolfgang Hoffmann and Pola Hoffmann. *Cigarette and Match Holder with Ashtray*, c.1930

Bottom: William Lescaze. *Desk Accessory*, 1932

Designed for the Philadelphia Savings Fund Society (P.S.F.S.) Building, Philadelphia, Pennsylvania

Opposite: Donald Deskey. *Table Lamp*, 1927

Left: Russel Wright. *Salt and Pepper Shakers*, c.1930

Center: William Lescaze. *Salt and Pepper Shakers*, c.1935

118 Right: Charles Sheeler. *Salt and Pepper Shakers*, 1935

Above: George Sakier. *Sink*, 1933

Overleaf left: Russel Wright. *Cocktail Shaker and Two Goblets*, c. 1931

Overleaf right: Ilonka Karasz. *Footed Bowls*, c. 1930

| Reuben Haley. "Ruba Rombic" Glassware, 1928

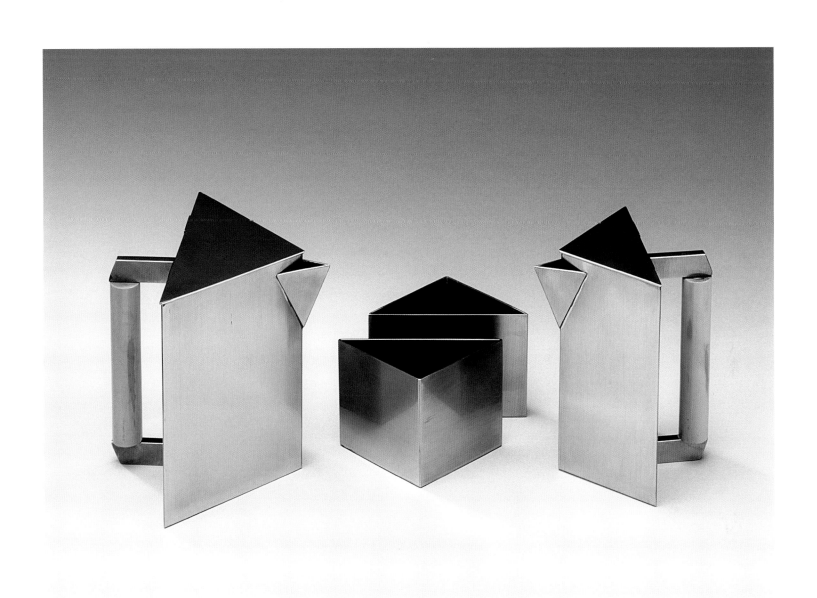

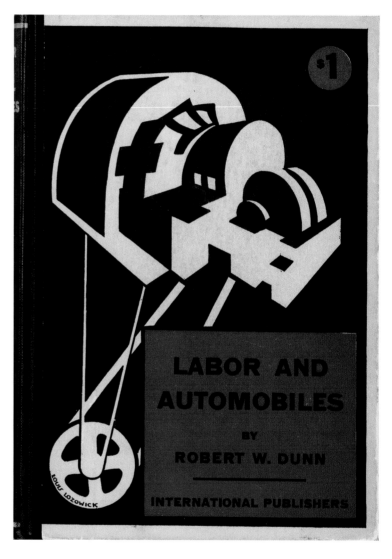

Left: F. V. Carpenter. *Cover for* Fortune *Magazine,* September 1932

Right: Louis Lozowick. *Cover for* Labor and Automobiles *(by Robert W. Dunn),* 1929

Opposite: Designer unknown. *Table Lamp,* c. 1935

STREAMLINED

If Art Deco came from France and geometric modernism from Germany, streamlining was identifiably American. The idea of speed captivated the nation. Ocean liners vied to set records for transatlantic crossings. Detroit turned out more and more powerful motorcars. Air travel became a reality, and fantasies of the future envisioned trips on rocket ships. Even a spring-driven contraption for pulverizing ice cubes with the pull of a trigger (page 135) masqueraded as a ray gun fit for a Buck Rogers or Flash Gordon, comic-book heroes whose interplanetary exploits could be followed on the radio or in Saturday morning movie serials.

Teardrop or bullet-shaped aerodynamic design was efficient in moving objects through space with the least air resistance, and hence it was appropriate for airplanes, automobiles, and railroad trains (fig. 20, page 29); but it also *looked* fast. And nothing symbolized the optimism of the new age better than speed. All sorts of stationary objects were given rounded corners, from meat slicers (page 134) and desk lamps (page 137), to furniture (pages 138, 139, 140, 141), interiors (fig. 25, page 33), and even buildings.

TO THE ADVANCEMENT OF MOTOR TRANSPORTATION

NORMAN BEL GEDDES © 1933

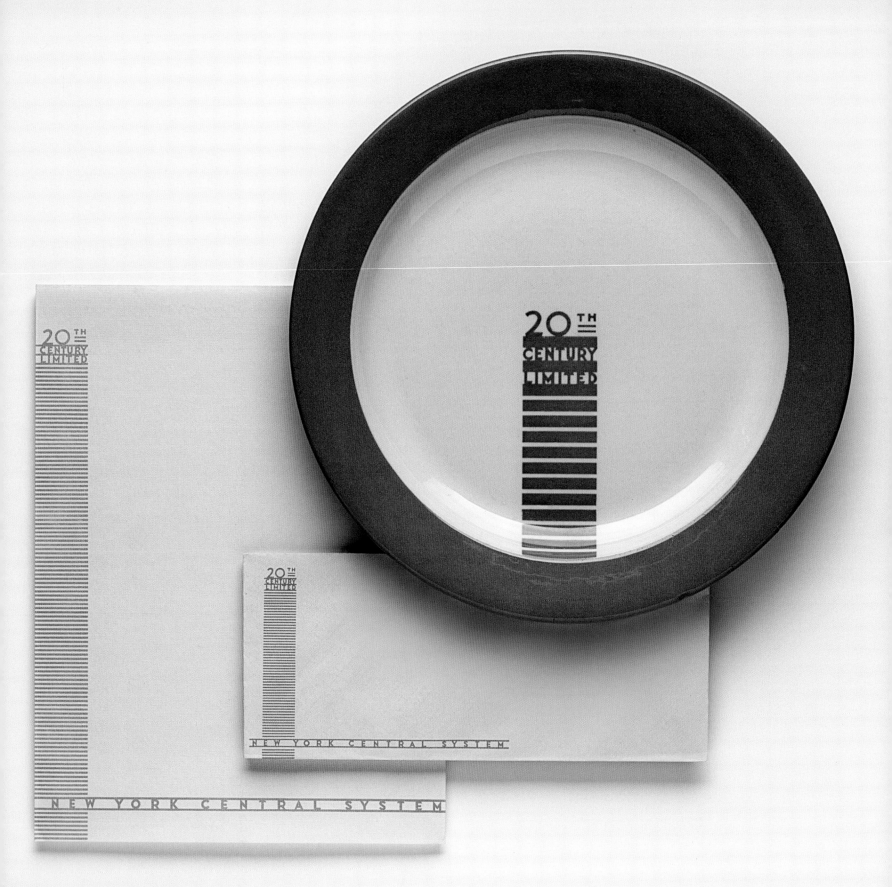

Above: Paolo Garretto. *Cover for* Fortune *Magazine*, August 1932
Opposite: Henry Dreyfuss. *Plate and Stationery*, 1938
Designed for the "20th Century Limited," New York Central Railroad

129

Above: Charles B. Falls. *Illustrations for* The Modern ABC Book, 1930

Opposite: John R. Morgan *"Waterwitch" Outboard Motor*, 1936

Harold L. Van Doren and John G. Ridcout. "Sno-Plane" Sled, 1934

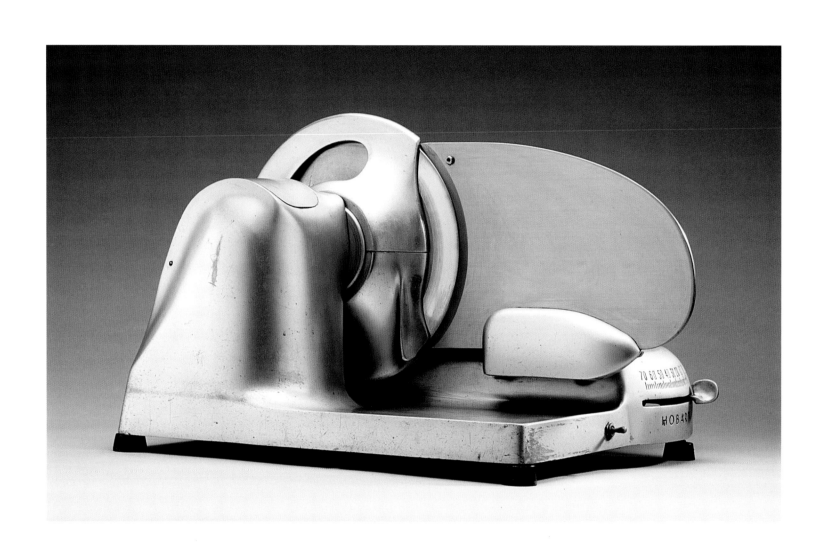

Egmont H. Arens and Theodore C. Brookhart. *"Streamliner" Meat Slicer*, designed 1940, manufactured from 1944

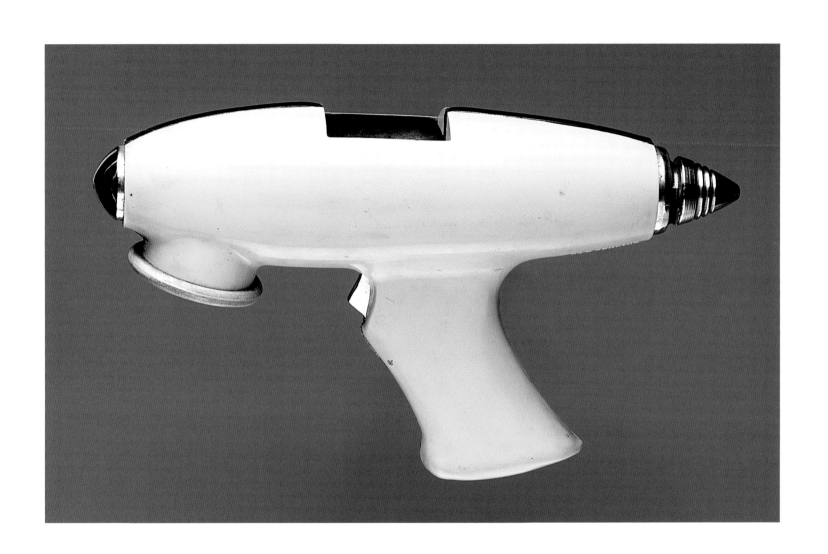

Paul T Frankl. *Lounge Chair, c. 1932*

Kem Weber. *"Airline"* Armchair, c.1934 | 139

Above: Gilbert Rohde. *Armchair*, c. 1930

Opposite: Norman Bel Geddes. *Dressing Table and Mirror*, 1932

Top: Gilbert Rohde. *Electric Clock*, c.1933

An example of this clock was shown in the 1934 "Machine Art" exhibition at the Museum of Modern Art, New York

Bottom: William Lescaze. *Desk Lamp*, 1932

Designed for the Philadelphia Savings Fund Society (P.S.F.S.) Building, Philadelphia, Pennsylvania

An example of this lamp was shown in the 1934 "Machine Art" exhibition at the Museum of Modern Art, New York

Opposite: Gilbert Rohde. *Electric Clock*, c.1933

RAMBUSCH
WALL URN
TYPE TF 360
OVER ALL HEIGHT 10¼"
TOTAL PROJECTION 10⅛"

300 WATT
R 40 FLOOD
OR R 40 SPOT

NOTE:
LOUVRES PLACED TO PERMIT FREE PASSAGE
OF UPWARD LIGHT ~ GIVING MAXIMUM EFFICIENCY
AND MINIMUM "BACK-SPLASH"

Above: Designer unknown. "TF-360" Theater Lighting Fixture and Design Drawing, c. 1935

Opposite: Peter Müller-Munk. "Normandie" Water Pitcher, 1935

B E Y O N D   M O D E R N I S

▶▶▶▶▶▶▶▶▶▶▶▶▶▶▶▶▶▶ During the 1930s, despite the Depression, life became easier for many Americans. Government-sponsored public-works projects built roads, dammed rivers, and brought electricity to large sections of the country (pages 147–150) and in so doing created a new audience for power-driven appliances. Electric refrigerators (page 155), vacuum cleaners (page 133), radios (page 151), toasters (page 153), and the like were no longer confined to urban centers.

As the market broadened, taste changed. The hard-edged modernism of the late 1920s and 1930s might still be admired, but it had never been endearing. Despite all the efforts to sell the style, in the end the majority of Americans preferred comfort to chic. Metal furniture was cold to the touch; wood, warm. Natural, textured materials—wool, sisal, cork—suited the increasingly informal American lifestyle better than such sleek materials as silk, rayon, and chrome.

The first shipment of the Finnish architect Alvar Aalto's bent plywood furniture was imported in 1936, and thereafter progressive architects began to prescribe his furniture for their interiors. Predictably, American designers responded with similar designs of their own.

Although the majority of people still chose period reproductions when furnishing their homes, the new wooden furniture, inspired by Scandinavian design, seemed far easier to live with than had tubular steel. By the end of the 1930s, the adjectives *moderne* and *modernistic* had both become pejorative and *modern* had taken on a new meaning. American modern had finally been domesticated.

BEALL

WASH DAY

RURAL ELECTRIFICATION ADMINISTRATION

148

Left: Lester Beall. *"Heat / Cold / Rural Electrification Administration"* Poster, 1937

Right: Lester Beall. *"Farm Work / Rural Electrification Administration"* Poster, 1937

Left: Lester Beall. *"Light / Rural Electrification Administration"* Poster, 1937
Right: Lester Beall. *"Running Water / Rural Electrification Administration"* Poster, 1937

Lester Beall. *"Radio / Rural Electrification Administration"* Poster, 1937

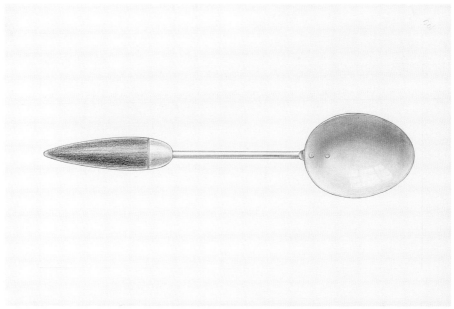

Top: Henry Dreyfuss. *Kitchen Utensils*, 1934

Bottom: Henry Dreyfuss. *Design Drawing for a Kitchen Spoon*, 1934

Above: J. Palin Thorley. *Refrigerator Pitcher*, 1940
Designed for the Westinghouse Electric Company
Overleaf left: Henry Dreyfuss. *Thermos Carafe and Tray*, 1935
Overleaf right: Ilonka Karasz. *"Lamelle" Tea Service*, c. 1934
A decorated variation of this service was shown at the 1934 exhibition
"Contemporary American Industrial Art" at The Metropolitan Museum of Art

Russel Wright. *"American Modern"* Dinnerware, 1937

Frank Lloyd Wright. *Desk and Chair*, c. 1936

Made for the S. C. Johnson and Son Administration Building, Racine, Wisconsin

Above: J. Robert F. Swanson with Saarinen-Swanson Group. *"Flexible Home Arrangements"* Nesting Tables, c. 1940

Opposite: Walter Dorwin Teague. *Desk Lamp*, 1939

164 | Isamu Noguchi. *"Radio Nurse"* Radio Transmitter, 1937

Top: Raymond Loewy. "Purma Special" Camera, 1934; Walter Dorwin Teague "Bantam Special" Camera, 1936

Bottom: Henry Dreyfuss. "Big Ben" Alarm Clock with Original Box, 1938

HORIZONS

A GLIMPSE
into the
NOT FAR-DISTANT FUTURE,
a future that will see many if not all of our present
notions of form cast into the discard——when, through
the influence of new design, most of the features of our
everyday life will take on new aspects for the greater
economy, efficiency, comfort and happiness of our lives.

NORMAN BEL GEDDES

Above: Norman Bel Geddes. *Cover for Horizons,* 1932

Opposite: Norman Bel Geddes. *"Patriot" Radio,* 1940

Checklist of the Exhibition

All works are either in the collection of The Metropolitan Museum of Art or are promised gifts to it, with the exception of those marked with a cross (+). An asterisk (*) indicates that the work will be shown at the Metropolitan Museum only. Due to the fragility of the textiles and graphic materials, only a portion of them will be on view at any given venue of the exhibition tour.

AMERICAN UNION OF DECORATIVE ARTISTS AND CRAFTSMEN (AUDAC)

Annual of American Design 1931, 1930
Publisher: Ives Washburn (New York, N.Y.)
H 12 1/4 x W 9 3/8" (31.1 x 23.8 cm)
Thomas J. Watson Library
page 69

EGMONT ARENS
(American, 1888–1966)
THEODORE C. BROOKHART
(American, 1898–1942)

"Streamliner" Meat Slicer, designed 1940, manufactured from 1944
Manufacturer: Hobart Manufacturing Company (Troy, Ohio)
Aluminum, steel, rubber
H 13 1/2 x W 21 x D 15" (34.3 x 53.3 x 38.1 cm)
John C. Waddell Collection, Promised Gift of John C. Waddell
page 134

RALPH BARTON
(American, 1891–1931)

"Americana Print: Gentlemen Prefer Blondes" Textile, 1926
Manufacturer: Stehli Silks Corporation (New York, N.Y.)
Printed silk, L 29 x W 37 3/4" (73.7 x 95.9 cm)
Gift of Stehli Silks Corporation, 1927 (27.149.11)
page 82

LESTER BEALL
(American, 1903–1969)

"Farm Work/Rural Electrification Administration" Poster, 1937
Silkscreen poster, H 40 x W 30" (101.6 x 76.2 cm)
John C. Waddell Collection, Promised Gift of John C. Waddell
page 148

"Heat/Cold/Rural Electrification Administration" Poster, 1937
Silkscreen poster, H 40 x W 30" (101.6 x 76.2 cm)
John C. Waddell Collection, Promised Gift of John C. Waddell
page 148

"Light/Rural Electrification Administration" Poster, 1937
Silkscreen poster, H 40 x W 30" (101.6 x 76.2 cm)
John C. Waddell Collection, Promised Gift of John C. Waddell
page 149

"Radio/Rural Electrification Administration" Poster, 1937
Silkscreen poster, H 40 x W 30" (101.6 x 76.2 cm)
John C. Waddell Collection, Promised Gift of John C. Waddell
page 150

"Running Water/Rural Electrification Administration" Poster, 1937
Silkscreen poster, H 40 x W 30" (101.6 x 76.2 cm)
John C. Waddell Collection, Promised Gift of John C. Waddell
page 149

"Wash Day/Rural Electrification Administration" Poster, 1937
Silkscreen poster, H 40 x W 30" (101.6 x 76.2 cm)
John C. Waddell Collection, Promised Gift of John C. Waddell
page 147

NORMAN BEL GEDDES
(American, 1893–1958)

Dressing Table, 1932
Manufacturer: Simmons Furniture Company (Chicago, Ill.)
Enameled and chrome-plated steel

H 29 5/8 x W 44 x D 19" (75.2 x 111.8 x 48.3 cm)
Gift of Paul F. Walter, 1984 (1984.263)
page 141

Mirror, 1932
Manufacturer: Simmons Furniture Company (Chicago, Ill.)
Glass, aluminum, enameled steel
H 26 x W 27 5/8 x D 6 5/8" (66 x 70.2 x 16.8 cm)
Purchase, Paul F. Walter Gift, 1985 (1985.165)
page 141

Horizons, 1932 +
Publisher: Little, Brown, and Company (Boston, Mass.)
Printed paper, H 10 1/2 x W 8 1/4" (26.7 x 21 cm)
Collection of John C. Waddell
page 166

Medals, 1933
Commemorating the twenty-fifth anniversary of General Motors
Manufacturer: Medallic Art Company (New York, N.Y.)
Silver, Each: Diam 3" (7.6 cm)
Gift of General Motors Corporation, 1933 (33.150.1, .2)
page 127

"Manhattan" Cocktail Set, 1937
Manufacturer: Revere Copper and Brass Company (Rome, N.Y.)
Chrome-plated brass
Shaker: H 13 x Diam 3 1/4" (33 x 8.3 cm)
Cups (each): H 4 1/2 x Diam 2 1/2" (11.4 x 6.4 cm)
Tray: L 14 1/2 x W 11 1/2" (36.8 x 29.2 cm)
John C. Waddell Collection, Gift of John C. Waddell, 1998
(1998.537.11ab–.18)
page 85

"Patriot" Radio, 1940
Manufacturer: Emerson Radio and Phonograph Corporation
(New York, N.Y.)
Catalin, H 8 x W 11 x D 5 1/2" (20.3 x 27.9 x 14 cm)
John C. Waddell Collection, Promised Gift of John C. Waddell
page 167

NORMAN BEL GEDDES
WORTHEN PAXTON
(American, 1905–1977)

"Soda King" Syphon Bottles, 1938
Manufacturer: Walter Kidde Sales Company (Bloomfield, N.J.)
Chrome-plated metal, brass, paint, rubber
Each: H 9 3/4 x Diam 4 3/8" (24.8 x 11.1 cm)
John C. Waddell Collection, Promised Gift of John C. Waddell
page 99

FREDERICK CARDER
(American, born England, 1863–1963)

Fork and Spoon, 1928–31
Manufacturer: Corning Glass Works, Steuben Division
(Corning, N.Y.)
Silver plate, glass
Fork: L 8" (20.3 cm)
Spoon: L 7 3/4" (19.7 cm)
John C. Waddell Collection, Gift of John C. Waddell, 1998
(1998.537.1, .2)
page 96

F. V. CARPENTER
(American, dates unknown)

Cover for *Fortune* Magazine, September 1932+
Printed paper, H 14 x W 11 1/2" (35.6 x 29.2 cm)
Collection of John C. Waddell
page 124

DONALD DESKEY
(American, 1894–1989)

Table Lamp, 1927
Manufacturer: Deskey-Vollmer (New York, N.Y.)
Chrome-plated metal, glass, H 12 1/4 x W 4 3/8 x D 5 5/8"
(31.1 x 11.1 x 14.3 cm)
John C. Waddell Collection, Promised Gift of John C. Waddell
page 117

Cigarette Box, c. 1927
Manufacturer: Deskey-Vollmer (New York, N.Y.)
Painted wood, silver leaf, H 4 1/8 x W 6 1/4 x D 3 5/8"
(10.5 x 15.9 x 9.2 cm)
John C. Waddell Collection, Promised Gift of John C. Waddell
page 66

Pamphlet Cover, 1928
Designed for the Gift and Art Shop, July 1928
Publisher: Geyer Publications, Andrew Geyer Inc. Publishers
(New York, N.Y.)
Printed paper, H 11 x W 8" (27.9 x 20.3 cm)
Anonymous Gift, 1999 (1999.432)
page 54

Table, c. 1928
Bakelite, extruded aluminum
H 21 3/8 x Diam 18" (54.3 x 45.7 cm)
Gift of Donald Deskey, 1987 (1987.361)
page 90

Console Table, 1932*
Designed for Radio City Music Hall, New York, N.Y.
Formica, aluminum
H 29 1/2 x W 24 x D 12" (74.9 x 61 x 30.5 cm)
John C. Waddell Collection, Promised Gift of John C. Waddell
page 92

"Singing Women" Carpet, 1932
Designed for the main auditorium of Radio City Music Hall,
New York, N.Y.
Wool, L 68 x W 65" (172.7 x 165.1 cm)
John C. Waddell Collection, Promised Gift of John C. Waddell
page 83

Table Lamp, c. 1934
Wood, chrome-plated metal
H 15 1/8 x Diam 11" (38.1 x 27.9 cm)
John C. Waddell Collection, Promised Gift of John C. Waddell
page 93

HENRY DREYFUSS
(American, 1904–1972)

Electric Toaster, 1932
Manufacturer: Birtman Electric Company (Chicago, Ill.)
Chrome-plated metal, plastic, glass
H 8 1/4 x W 7 7/8 x D 4 5/8" (21 x 20 x 11.7 cm)
John C. Waddell Collection, Promised Gift of John C. Waddell
page 153

Kitchen Utensils, 1934
Manufacturer: The Washburn Company (Worcester, Mass.)
Metal, painted wood
Potato Masher: L 10 1/4 x W 4 x D 3" (26 x 10.2 x 7.6 cm)
Spoon: L 11 3/4 x W 2 5/8" (29.8 x 6.7 cm)
John C. Waddell Collection, Gift of John C. Waddell, 1998
(1998.537.5, .6)
page 154

Design Drawing for a Kitchen Spoon, 1934
Graphite and colored pencil on paper
H 14 3/4 x W 9 3/4" (37.5 x 24.8 cm)
John C. Waddell Collection, Gift of John C. Waddell, 1998
(1998.537.7)
page 154

Thermos Carafe and Tray, 1935
Manufacturer: The American Thermos Bottle Company
(Norwich, Conn.)
Enamel, aluminum, cork
Thermos: H 5 7/8 x W 6 x D 5" (14.9 x 15.2 x 12.7 cm)
Tray: H 1/4 x W 9 1/4 x D 6 5/8" (.64 x 23.5 x 16.8 cm)
John C. Waddell Collection, Gift of John C. Waddell, 1998
(1998.537.3ab, .4)
page 156

Thermos Bottle and Cups, 1937
Manufacturer: The American Thermos Bottle Company
(Norwich, Conn.)
Metal, glass, plastic, paint, cork
H 13 3/4 x W 4 x D 3 7/8" (34.9 x 10.2 x 9.8 cm)
John C. Waddell Collection, Gift of John C. Waddell, 1998
(1998.537.8a–f)
page 98

"Big Ben" Alarm Clock with Original Box, 1938
Manufacturer: General Time Instruments Corporation,
Westclox Company Division (La Salle, Ill.)
Metal, chrome-plated metal, enamel; printed cardboard
Clock: H 5 3/4 x W 5 1/8 x D 3" (14.6 x 13 x 7.6 cm)
Box: H 4 x W 6 1/8 x D 6 1/2" (10.2 x 15.6 x 16.5 cm)
John C. Waddell Collection, Promised Gift of John C. Waddell
page 165

Plate, 1938
Designed for the "20th Century Limited," New York
Central Railroad
Manufacturer: Buffalo China (Buffalo, N.Y.)
Ceramic, Diam 10 5/8" (27 cm)
John C. Waddell Collection, Promised Gift of John C. Waddell
page 128

Writing Paper and Envelope, 1938
Designed for the "20th Century Limited," New York
Central Railroad
Printed paper
Writing paper: H 10 1/2 x W 8" (26.7 x 20.3 cm)
Envelope: H 3 7/8 x W 9" (9.8 x 22.9 cm)
John C. Waddell Collection, Promised Gift of John C. Waddell
page 128

HELEN DRYDEN
(American, 1887–1934)

"Americana Print: Accessories" Textile, 1926
Manufacturer: Stehli Silks Corporation (New York, N.Y.)
Printed silk, L 37 x W 39" (94 x 99.1 cm)
Gift of Stehli Silks Corporation, 1927 (27.149.7)
page 80

HELEN A. HUGHES DULANY
(American, 1895–1991)

Coffee Service, 1934
Stainless steel, Bakelite
Large pot: H 5 3/8 x W 5 3/8 x D 5" (13.7 x 13.7 x 12.7 cm)
Small pot: H 5 3/8 x W 3 7/8 x D 4" (13.7 x 9.8 x 10.2 cm)
Sugar: H 2 5/8 x W 3 3/4 x D 1 7/8" (6.7 x 9.5 x 4.8 cm)
Creamer: H 2 5/8 x W 3 3/4 x D 1 7/8" (6.7 x 9.5 x 4.8 cm)
John C. Waddell Collection, Promised Gift of John C. Waddell
page 123

W. A. DWIGGINS
(American, 1880–1956)

The Architect and the Industrial Arts, 1929
Catalogue of the eleventh annual exhibition of contemporary
American design held at The Metropolitan Museum of Art,
February 12–September 2, 1929
Publisher: The Metropolitan Museum of Art and The Plandome
Press, Inc. (New York, N.Y.)
Printed paper, H 8 5/8 x W 5 5/8" (21.9 x 14.3 cm)
Thomas J. Watson Library
page 76

The Power of Print—and Men (by Thomas Dreier), 1936+
Publisher: Mergenthaler Linotype Company (Brooklyn, N.Y.)
Printed paper, H 9 7/8 x W 7 3/8" (25.1 x 18.7 cm)
Collection of John C. Waddell
page 76

CHARLES B. FALLS
(American, 1874–1960)

"Americana Print: Pegs" Textile, 1927
Manufacturer: Stehli Silks Corporation (New York, N.Y.)
Printed silk, L 29 1/4 x W 38 1/2" (74.3 x 97.8 cm)
Gift of Stehli Silks Corporation, 1927 (27.243.2)
page 75

Illustrations for *The Modern ABC Book*, 1930+
Publisher: The John Day Company (New York, N.Y.)
Printed paper, H 12 1/4 x W 9 3/8" (31.1 x 23.8 cm)
Collection of John C. Waddell
page 130

ROBERT FAWCETT
(American, born England, 1903–1967)

Epitaph (by Theodore Dreiser), 1929
Publisher: Heron Press Inc. (New York, N.Y.)
Leather, silver and gold leaf
H 11 3/4 x W 9" (29.8 x 22.9 cm)
John C. Waddell Collection, Gift of John C. Waddell, 1998
(1998.537.9)
page 63

HUGH FERRISS
(American, 1889–1962)

The Metropolis of Tomorrow, 1929
Publisher: Ives Washburn (New York, N.Y.)
H 12 1/4 x W 9 1/2" (31.1 x 24.1 cm)
Thomas J. Watson Library
page 51

PAUL T. FRANKL
(American, born Austria, 1887–1958)

"Skyscraper" Bookcase, c. 1927
Maple, Bakelite
H 79 7/8 x W 34 3/8 x D 18 7/8" (202.9 x 87.3 x 47.9 cm)
Purchase, Theodore R. Gamble Jr. Gift, in honor of his
mother, Mrs. Theodore Robert Gamble, 1982 (1982.30ab)
page 53

"Skyscraper" Desk, c. 1927 1
Wood, Formica
H 44 7/8 x W 55 3/8 x D 31 1/4" (114 x 140.7 x 79.4 cm)
Collection of John C. Waddell
page 52

Form and Re-form: A Practical Handbook of Modern Interiors,
1930
Publisher: Harper and Brothers (New York, N.Y.)
H 8 5/8 x W 6" (21.9 x 15.2 cm)
John C. Waddell Collection, Gift of John C. Waddell, 1998
(1998.537.10)
page 49

Lounge Chair, c. 1932*+
Wood, cork, monk's cloth upholstery
H 24 1/2 x W 36 x D 41" (61.5 x 91.4 x 104.1 cm)
Collection of John C. Waddell
page 138

EDWIN W. FUERST
(American, 1903–1988)

"Knickerbocker" Glassware, 1939
Manufacturer: Libbey Glass Company (Toledo, Ohio)
Glass
Decanter: H 11 x Diam 3 7/8" (27.9 x 9.8 cm)
Cordial glass: H 3 3/8 x Diam 2 1/4" (8.6 x 5.7 cm)
Cocktail glass: H 4 7/8 x Diam 2 1/2" (12.4 x 6.4 cm)
Water glass: H 5 3/4 x Diam 2 3/4" (14.6 x 7 cm)
Sherbet bowl: H 2 3/8 x Diam 4 3/8" (6 x 11.1 cm)
John C. Waddell Collection, Gift of John C. Waddell, 1998
(1998.537.33ab–.37)
page 100

PAOLO GARRETTO
(Italian, 1903–1989)

Cover for *Fortune* Magazine, August 1932+
Printed paper, H 14 x W 11 1/2" (35.6 x 29.2 cm)
Collection of John C. Waddell
page 129

KNEELAND L. ("RUZZIE") GREEN
(American, 1892–1956)

"Americana Print: It" Textile, 1927
Manufacturer: Stehli Silks Corporation (New York, N.Y.)
Printed silk, L 29 x W 38 1/2" (73.7 x 97.8 cm)
Gift of Stehli Silks Corporation, 1927 (27.243.6)
page 81

"Americana Print: Cheerio" Textile, 1927
Manufacturer: Stehli Silks Corporation (New York, N.Y.)
Printed silk, L 24 3/4 x W 38 1/2" (62.9 x 97.8 cm)
Gift of Stehli Silks Corporation, 1927 (27.243.7)
page 81

LURELLE GUILD
(American, 1898–1985)

Coffee Maker, 1932
Manufacturer: Aluminum Company of America, Wear-Ever
Aluminum Inc. Division (New Kensington, Penn.)
Aluminum, composition
H 10 ³/₄ x W 9 ¹/₄ x D 4 ¹/₄" (27.3 x 23.5 x 10.8 cm)
John C. Waddell Collection, Gift of John C. Waddell, 1998
(1998.537.20a–d)
page 152

Footed Bowl, 1934
Manufacturer: Aluminum Company of America, Kensington Inc.
Division (New Kensington, Penn.)
Aluminum, glass, H 5 ¹/₂ x Diam 13 ³/₄" (14 x 34.9 cm)
John C. Waddell Collection, Promised Gift of John C. Waddell
page 105

Cocktail Shaker, c. 1934
Manufacturer: International Silver Company, Wallace Silver
Plate Company Division (Meriden, Conn.)
Metal, enamel, lacquered wood
H 15 ³/₄ x Diam 3 ⁵/₈" (40 x 9.2 cm)
John C. Waddell Collection, Gift of John C. Waddell, 1998
(1998.537.19a–c)
page 62

"Electrolux, Model 30" Vacuum Cleaner, 1937+
Manufacturer: Electrolux Corporation (Dover, Del.)
Chrome-plated steel, aluminum, vinyl, rubber
H 8 ¹/₂ x L 23 x W 7 ³/₄" (21.6 x 58.4 x 19.7 cm)
Collection of John C. Waddell
page 133

REUBEN HALEY
(American, 1872–1933)

"Ruba Rombic" Glassware, 1928
Manufacturer: Consolidated Lamp and Glass Company, Art
Glassware Division (Coraopolis, Penn.)
Glass
page 122

Vase: H 9 ¹/₄ x Diam 7" (23.5 x 17.8 cm)
Purchase, Theodore R. Gamble Jr. Gift in honor of his mother,
Mrs. Theodore Robert Gamble, 1986 (1986.413.2)

Jug: H 8 x W 6 ¹/₂ x D 9" (20.3 x 16.5 x 22.9 cm)
Bowl: H 4 ¹/₂ x Diam 8 ¹/₂" (11.4 x 21.6 cm)
Plate: H 1 x Diam 10 ⁵/₈" (2.5 x 27 cm)
Tumbler: H 4 x Diam 3" (10.2 x 7.6 cm)
Glass: H 6 x Diam 3 ³/₈" (15.2 x 8.6 cm)
John C. Waddell Collection, Gift of John C. Waddell, 1998
(1998.537.21–.25)

Liqueur glass: H 2 ³/₄ x Diam 2" (7 x 5.1 cm)
John C. Waddell Collection, Gift of John C. Waddell, 1999
(1999.430)

JOHN HELD, JR.
(American, 1889–1958)

"Americana Print: Collegiate" Textile, 1926
Manufacturer: Stehli Silks Corporation (New York, N.Y.)
Printed silk, L 38 x W 39" (96.5 x 99.1 cm)
Gift of Stehli Silks Corporation, 1927 (27.149.8)
page 78

"Americana Print: 100 Per Cent" Textile, 1926
Manufacturer: Stehli Silks Corporation (New York, N.Y.)
Printed silk, L 41 x W 38 ³/₄" (104.1 x 98.4 cm)
Gift of Stehli Silks Corporation, 1927 (27.149.9)
page 78

"Americana Print: Rhapsody" Textile, 1927
Manufacturer: Stehli Silks Corporation (New York, N.Y.)
Printed silk, L 12 ⁵/₈ x W 39 ¹/₂" (32.1 x 100.3 cm)
Gift of Stehli Silks Corporation, 1927 (27.149.10)
page 79

WOLFGANG HOFFMANN
(American, born Austria, 1900–1969)
POLA HOFFMANN
(American, born Poland, 1902–?)

Cigarette and Match Holder with Ashtray, c. 1930
Manufacturer: Early American Pewter Company (Boston, Mass.)
Pewter, H 2 x W 4 x D 2 ¹/₄" (5.1 x 10.2 x 5.7 cm)
John C. Waddell Collection, Promised Gift of John C. Waddell
page 117

FRANK G. HOLMES
(American, 1878–1954)

Vase, c. 1934
An example of this vase was shown in the 1934 "Machine Art"
exhibition at the Museum of Modern Art, New York
Manufacturer: Lenox, Inc. (Trenton, N.J.)
Porcelain, H 11 ³/₈ x Diam 3 ¹/₂" (28.9 x 8.9 cm)
John C. Waddell Collection, Promised Gift of John C. Waddell
page 112

ILONKA KARASZ
(American, born Hungary, 1896–1981)

Rug, 1928
Shown in the nursery Karasz designed for the 1928
American Designers' Gallery Inc. exhibition, New York
Cotton, wool, L 107 x W 109 ¹/₂" (271.8 x 278.2 cm)
Purchase, Theodore R. Gamble Jr. Gift, in honor of his mother,
Mrs. Theodore Robert Gamble, 1983 (1983.228.3)
page 70

Leaflet, 1928
Designed for the 1928 American Designers' Gallery Inc.
exhibition, New York
Publisher: American Designers' Gallery Inc. (New York, N.Y.)
Printed paper
Full sheet: H 20 ³/₈ x W 14 ³/₄" (51.8 x 37.5 cm)
John C. Waddell Collection, Promised Gift of John C. Waddell
page 68

Coffee and Tea Service, c. 1928
Manufacturer: Paye and Baker Manufacturing Company
(North Attleboro, Mass.)
Electroplated nickel silver, walnut
page 58

Coffee pot: H 7 x W 6 ¹/₂ x D 4" (17.8 x 16.5 x 10.2 cm)
Teapot: H 4 ³/₄ x W 6 ¹/₄ x D 4" (12.1 x 15.9 x 10.2 cm)
Creamer: H 2 ¹/₂ x W 6 ¹/₈ x D 4" (6.4 x 15.6 x 10.2 cm)
Sugar: H 3 ³/₄ x W 6 ⁵/₈ x D 4" (9.5 x 16.8 x 10.2 cm)
Purchase, Theodore R. Gamble Jr. Gift, in honor of his mother,
Mrs. Theodore Robert Gamble, 1979 (1979.219.1ab–.4ab)

Water pot: H 3 ³/₄ x W 6 ¹/₄ x D 4" (9.5 x 15.9 x 10.2 cm)
John C. Waddell Collection, Gift of John C. Waddell, 1998
(1998.537.26)

Footed Bowl, c. 1930
Manufacturer: Paye and Baker Manufacturing Company
(North Attleboro, Mass.)
Electroplated nickel silver, H 2 ³/₈ x Diam 4 ¹/₄" (6 x 10.8 cm)
John C. Waddell Collection, Promised Gift of John C. Waddell
page 121

Footed Bowl, c. 1930
Manufacturer: Paye and Baker Manufacturing Company
(North Attleboro, Mass.)
Electroplated nickel silver, H 1 ³/₄ x Diam 2 ⁷/₈" (4.4 x 7.3 cm)
Purchase, Theodore R. Gamble Jr. Gift, in honor of his mother,
Mrs. Theodore Robert Gamble, 1983 (1983.228.1)
page 121

"Lamelle" Tea Service, c. 1934
A decorated variation of this service was shown in the
1934 exhibition "Contemporary American Industrial
Art" at The Metropolitan Museum of Art
Manufacturer: Buffalo China (Buffalo, N.Y.)
Earthenware
Teapot: H 7 x W 6 ³/4 x D 6 ¹/2" (17.8 x 17.1 x 16.5 cm)
Stand: H 3 ¹/2 x Diam 5 ¹/4" (8.9 x 13.3 cm)
Candleholder: H 1 ¹/2 x W 3 ³/8 x D 2 ⁵/8" (3.8 x 8.6 x 6.7 cm)
Sugar: H 4 x W 6 x D 5" (10.2 x 15.2 x 12.7 cm)
Creamer: H 2 ⁷/8 x W 6 ³/4 x D 5" (7.3 x 17.1 x 12.7 cm)
Cup: H 2 ⁷/8 x W 4 ⁷/8 x D 4" (7.3 x 12.4 x 10.2 cm)
Saucer: Diam 6" (15.2 cm)
Plate: Diam 10 ³/4" (27.3 cm)
Purchase, Theodore R. Gamble Jr. Gift, in honor of
his mother, Mrs. Theodore Robert Gamble, 1983
(1983.178.1ab–.7, .11)
page 157

CLARENCE KARSTADT
(American, 1902–1968)

"Silvertone" Radio, 1938
Manufacturer: Sears, Roebuck and Company (Chicago, Ill.)
Bakelite, H 6 ¹/2 x L 11 ³/4 x D 6 ¹/2" (16.5 x 29.8 x 16.5 cm)
John C. Waddell Collection, Promised Gift of John C. Waddell
page 151

CLAYTON KNIGHT
(American, 1891–1969)

"Americana Print: Manhattan" Textile, 1925
Manufacturer: Stehli Silks Corporation (New York, N.Y.)
Printed silk, L 24 ³/4 x W 25 ¹/4" (62.9 x 64.1 cm)
Gift of Stehli Silks Corporation, 1927 (27.150.3)
page 47

WILLIAM LESCAZE
(American, born Switzerland, 1896–1969)

Desk Lamp, 1932
Designed for the Philadelphia Savings Fund Society (P.S.F.S.)
Building, Philadelphia, Penn.
An example of this lamp was shown in the 1934 "Machine Art"
exhibition at the Museum of Modern Art, New York
Manufacturer: Kurt Versen (New York, N.Y.)
Chrome-plated metal, paint
H 15 ⁵/8 x W 18 ¹/2 x D 7 ¹/2" (39.7 x 47 x 19.1 cm)
John C. Waddell Collection, Promised Gift of John C. Waddell
page 142

Desk Accessory, 1932⁺
Designed for the Philadelphia Savings Fund Society (P.S.F.S.)
Building, Philadelphia, Penn.
Chrome-plated brass, H 3 ¹/2 x Diam 5 ¹/2" (8.9 x 14 cm)
Collection of John C. Waddell
page 117

Salt and Pepper Shakers, c. 1935
Manufacturer: Revere Copper and Brass Company (Rome, N.Y.)
Metal, plastic, Each: H 1 ³/4 x W ⁵/8 x D 2" (4.5 x 1.59 x 5.1 cm)
John C. Waddell Collection, Gift of John C. Waddell, 1998
(1998.537.27ab)
page 118

PAUL LOBEL
(American, born Romania, 1899–1983)

Tea Service, 1934
Exhibited at the 1934 exhibition "Contemporary American
Industrial Art" at The Metropolitan Museum of Art
Manufacturer: International Silver Company, Wilcox Silverplate
Company Division (Meriden, Conn.)
Silver plate, wood
Tray: H 1 x W 18 x D 8 ¹/8" (2.5 x 45.8 x 20.6 cm)
Teapot: H 6 x W 6 x D 8 ¹/4" (15.2 x 15.2 x 21 cm)
Sugar bowl: H 3 ⁷/8 x W 4 x D 5 ³/8" (9.9 x 10.2 x 13.7 cm)
Creamer: H 4 x W 4 x D 5 ¹/2" (10.2 x 10.2 x 14 cm)
Gift of M. H. Lobel and C. H. Lobel, 1983 (1983.493.1–.4)
page 107

RAYMOND LOEWY
(American, born France, 1893–1986)

"Purma Special" Camera, 1934
Manufacturer: Purma Camera, Ltd. (England)
Plastic, acrylic, H 2 ⁷/8 x L 6 x D 2 ¹/8" (7.3 x 15.2 x 5.4 cm)
John C. Waddell Collection, Promised Gift of John C. Waddell
page 165

LOUIS LOZOWICK
(American, born Ukraine, 1892–1973)

Labor and Automobiles (by Robert W. Dunn), 1929⁺
Publisher: International Publishers Company, Inc.
(New York, N.Y.)
Printed paper, H 7 ⁷/8 x W 5 ¹/2" (20 x 14 cm)
Collection of John C. Waddell
page 124

JOHN R. MORGAN
(American, dates unknown)

"Waterwitch" Outboard Motor, 1936
Manufacturer: Sears, Roebuck and Company (Chicago, Ill.)
Steel, aluminum, rubber, H 37 x W 16 x D 24" (94 x 40.6 x 61 cm)
John C. Waddell Collection, Gift of John C. Waddell, 1998
(1998.537.28)
page 131

PETER MÜLLER-MUNK
(American, born Germany, 1904–1967)

Tea Service, 1931
Silver, ivory
Teapot on stand: H 10 ¹/8 x W 9 ¹/4 x D 6 ⁷/8" (25.7 x 23.5 x 17.5 cm)
Water pot: H 8 x W 9 ⁵/8 x D 2 ³/4" (20.3 x 24.4 x 7 cm)
Sugar: H 5 x W 7 ³/4 x D 3 ¹/4" (12.7 x 19.7 x 8.3 cm)
Creamer: H 4 ¹/2 x W 6 ¹/4 x D 2 ¹/4" (11.4 x 15.9 x 5.7 cm)
Tray: H 1 x W 24 ³/4 x D 13 ³/4" (2.5 x 62.9 x 34.9 cm)
Gift of Mr. and Mrs. Herbert R. Isenburger, 1978
(1978.439.1–.5)
page 39

"Normandie" Water Pitcher, 1935
Manufacturer: Revere Copper and Brass Company (Rome, N.Y.)
Chrome-plated brass, H 12 x W 3 x D 9 ³/8" (30.5 x 7.6 x 23.8 cm)
Anonymous Gift, 1989 (1989.394)
page 145

ISAMU NOGUCHI
(American, 1904–1988)

"Radio Nurse" Radio Transmitter, 1937
Manufacturers: Zenith Radio Corporation (Chicago, Ill.),
Chicago Molded Products Corporation (Chicago, Ill.),
and Kurz-Kasch, Inc. (Dayton, Ohio)
Bakelite, H 8 x W 6 ¹/2 x D 6 ¹/2" (20.3 x 16.5 x 16.5 cm)
John C. Waddell Collection, Promised Gift of John C. Waddell
page 164

WILBER L. ORME
(American, 1889–1972)

"Pristine Table Architecture" Series Candleholders, 1938
Manufacturer: Cambridge Glass Company (Cambridge, Ohio)
Glass, Each: H 5 ³/8 x W 5 ¹/4 x D 1 ³/4" (13.7 x 13.3 x 4.5 cm)
John C. Waddell Collection, Promised Gift of John C. Waddell
pages 56–57

PETER PFISTERER
(American, born Switzerland, 1907–?)

Table Lamp, c. 1937
Chrome-plated and enameled metal, wood, glass
H 6 3/4 x L 13 5/8 x W 3 1/2" (17.1 x 34.6 x 8.9 cm)
John C. Waddell Collection, Promised Gift of John C. Waddell
page 113

RUTH REEVES
(American, 1892–1966)

"Figures with Still Life" Wall Hanging, 1930
Designed for W. & J. Sloane, New York, N.Y.
Block-printed cotton velvet, L 91 3/8 x W 46" (233 x 166.8 cm)
Bequest of James Stubblebine, 1987 (1987.473.5)
page 71

LOUIS W. RICE
(American, dates unknown)

"Skyscraper" Cocktail Shaker, 1928
Manufacturer: Bernard Rice's Sons, Inc. (New York, N.Y.)
Electroplated nickel silver
H 11 1/8 x W 7 1/4 x D 4 1/8" (28.3 x 18.4 x 10.5 cm)
John C. Waddell Collection, Promised Gift of John C. Waddell
page 48

GILBERT ROHDE
(American, 1894–1944)

Armchair, c. 1930
Manufacturer: The Troy Sunshade Company (Troy, Ohio)
Chrome-plated steel, painted wood, new upholstery
H 34 3/8 x W 23 x D 28 1/2" (87.3 x 58.4 x 72.4 cm)
Gifts in memory of Emil Blasberg, 1978 (1978.492.3)
page 140

Desk Lamp, 1933
Manufacturer: Mutual-Sunset Lamp Manufacturing Company,
Inc. (Brooklyn, N.Y.)
Chrome-plated steel, brass
H 7 x L 14 x W 2 1/4" (17.8 x 35.6 x 5.7 cm)
John C. Waddell Collection, Promised Gift of John C. Waddell
page 137

Electric Clock, c. 1933
Manufacturer: Herman Miller Clock Company (Zeeland, Mich.)
Chrome-plated and enameled metal, glass
H 6 1/2 x W 11 1/2 x D 5" (16.5 x 29.2 x 12.7 cm)
John C. Waddell Collection, Promised Gift of John C. Waddell
page 114

Electric Clock, c. 1933
Manufacturer: Herman Miller Clock Company (Zeeland, Mich.)
Chrome-plated metal, glass
H 12 1/8 x W 12 1/2 x D 3 1/2" (30.8 x 31.8 x 8.9 cm)
John C. Waddell Collection, Promised Gift of John C. Waddell
page 143

Electric Clock, c. 1933
An example of this clock was shown in the 1934 "Machine Art"
exhibition at the Museum of Modern Art, New York
Manufacturer: Herman Miller Clock Company (Zeeland, Mich.)
Chrome-plated metal, glass
H 10 3/4 x W 10 x D 3 1/2" (27.3 x 25.4 x 8.9 cm)
John C. Waddell Collection, Promised Gift of John C. Waddell
page 142

HERMAN ROSSE
(American, born Netherlands, 1887–1965)

Dining Room Accessories, 1928
Exhibited in the dining room Rosse designed for the 1928
American Designers' Gallery Inc. exhibition, New York
Monel metal
Covered tureen: H 5 1/2 x Diam 10 1/4" (14 x 26 cm)
Covered urn: H 8 x Diam 5 1/4" (20.3 x 13.3 cm)
Tall vase: H 9 3/4 x Diam 4" (24.8 x 10.2 cm)
Planter: H 5 1/8 x W 11 3/4 x D 6 7/8" (13 x 29.8 cm)
Promised Gift of S. Helena Rosse Trust
page 86

ELIEL SAARINEN
(American, born Finland, 1873–1950)

Knife, 1929+
Designed for the 1929 exhibition "The Architect and the
Industrial Arts" at The Metropolitan Museum of Art, New York
Manufacturer: International Silver Company (Meriden, Conn.)
Silver, L 9 1/4" (23.5 cm)
Collection of John C. Waddell
page 44

Design Drawing for a Knife, 1929+
Pencil on paper, H 3 x W 11" (7.6 x 27.9 cm)
Collection of John C. Waddell
page 44

Centerpiece, c. 1929+
A variant of this design was shown in the 1929 exhibition
"The Architect and the Industrial Arts" at The Metropolitan
Museum of Art, New York
Manufacturer: International Silver Company, Wilcox
Silver Plate Company Division (Meriden, Conn.)
Silver, H 6 5/8 x Diam 15" (16.8 x 38.1 cm)
Collection of John C. Waddell
page 45

Tea and Coffee Urn and Tray, c. 1934
A variant of this design in silver plate was exhibited at the
1934 exhibition "Contemporary American Industrial Art"
at The Metropolitan Museum of Art
Manufacturer: International Silver Company, Wilcox
Silver Plate Company Division (Meriden, Conn.)
Electroplated nickel silver, brass, Bakelite
Urn: H 14 1/2 x W 7 3/4 x D 11" (36.8 x 19.7 x 27.9 cm)
Tray: Diam 17 1/2" (44.5 cm)
Purchase, Mr. and Mrs. Ronald Saarinen Swanson and John C.
Waddell Gifts, and Gift of Susan Dwight Bliss, by exchange,
1999 (1999.271.1a–c, .2)
page 106

GEORGE SAKIER
(American, 1897–1988)

"Lotus" Vases, 1928
Manufacturer: Fostoria Glass Company (Moundsville, W.V.)
Glass
Clear vase: H 12 3/4 x Diam 5" (32.4 x 12.7 cm)
Black vase: H 6 1/4 x Diam 2 1/2" (15.9 x 6.4 cm)
Yellow vase: H 9 3/8 x Diam 3 5/8" (23.8 x 9.2 cm)
John C. Waddell Collection, Promised Gift of John C. Waddell
page 59

Sink, 1933
Manufacturer: American Radiator and Standard Sanitary
Corporation (New York, N.Y.)
Porcelain, chrome-plated metal
H 34 x W 29 x D 19 1/2" (86.4 x 73.7 x 49.5 cm)
John C. Waddell Collection, Gift of John C. Waddell, 1998
(1998.537.29)
page 119

"Spool" Vase, 1937
Manufacturer: Fostoria Glass Company (Moundsville, W.V.)
Glass, H 5 1/4 x Diam 6 1/2" (13.3 x 16.5 cm)
John C. Waddell Collection, Promised Gift of John C. Waddell
page 103

EUGENE SCHOEN
(American, 1880–1957)

Etagère, 1929
Bakelite, bronze, chestnut
H 46 3/4 x W 51 x D 14 1/4" (118.7 x 129.5 x 36.2 cm)
Purchase, Robert and Meryl Meltzer Fund Gift, 1984
(1984.320)
page 55

CHARLES SHEELER
(American, 1883–1965)

Salt and Pepper Shakers, 1935
Aluminum, Each: H 1 1/2 x W 1 x D 1" (3.8 x 2.5 x 2.5 cm)
John C. Waddell Collection, Gift of John C. Waddell, 1998
(1998.537.30ab)
page 118

EDWARD J. STEICHEN
(American, born Luxembourg, 1879–1973)

"Americana Print: Moth Balls and Sugar" Textile, 1926
Manufacturer: Stehli Silks Corporation (New York, N.Y.)
Printed silk, L 36 1/2 x W 38 1/4" (92.7 x 97.2 cm)
Gift of Stehli Silks Corporation, 1927 (27.149.1)
page 72

"Americana Print: Sugar Lumps" Textile, 1926
Manufacturer: Stehli Silks Corporation (New York, N.Y.)
Printed silk, L 36 1/2 x W 40 3/4" (92.7 x 103.5 cm)
Gift of Stehli Silks Corporation, 1927 (27.149.3)
page 72

"Americana Print: Matches and Matchboxes" Textile, 1926
Manufacturer: Stehli Silks Corporation (New York, N.Y.)
Printed silk, L 36 1/4 x W 41" (92.1 x 104.1 cm)
Gift of Stehli Silks Corporation, 1927 (27.149.4)
page 73

"Americana Print: Buttons and Thread" Textile, 1927
Manufacturer: Stehli Silks Corporation (New York, N.Y.)
Printed silk, L 38 1/4 x W 26 1/2" (97.2 x 67.3 cm)
Gift of Stehli Silks Corporation, 1927 (27.243.8)
page 72

"Americana Print: Thread" Textile, 1927
Manufacturer: Stehli Silks Corporation (New York, N.Y.)
Printed silk, L 27 3/4 x W 38 3/4" (70.5 x 98.4 cm)
Gift of Stehli Silks Corporation, 1927 (27.243.9)
page 72

J. ROBERT F. SWANSON
(American, 1900–1981)
with Saarinen-Swanson Group

"Flexible Home Arrangements" Nesting Tables, c. 1940
Manufacturer: Johnson Furniture Company (Grand Rapids, Mich.)
Maple, stainless steel, Greatest H 18 x Greatest W 30 x
Greatest D 18 1/2" (45.7 x 76.2 x 47 cm)
John C. Waddell Collection, Promised Gift of John C. Waddell
page 163

WALTER DORWIN TEAGUE
(American, 1883–1960)

Camera and Box, 1930
Manufacturer: Eastman Kodak Company (Rochester, N.Y.)
Metal, lacquer
Camera: H 2 3/8 x L 8 7/8 x W 4 3/8" (6 x 22.5 x 11.1 cm)
Box: H 3 1/2 x L 8 x W 6 1/2" (8.9 x 20.3 x 16.5 cm)
John C. Waddell Collection, Gift of John C. Waddell, 1998
(1998.537.38, .39a–c)
page 65

Bowl, 1932
Manufacturer: Corning Glass Works, Steuben Division
(Corning, N.Y.)
Glass, H 2 5/8 x Diam 16" (6.7 x 40.6 cm)
John C. Waddell Collection, Promised Gift of John C. Waddell
page 102

Vase, 1932
Manufacturer: Corning Glass Works, Steuben Division
(Corning, N.Y.)
Glass, H 6 3/8 x Diam 7 3/8" (16.2 x 18.7 cm)
John C. Waddell Collection, Promised Gift of John C. Waddell
page 104

Vase, 1932
Manufacturer: Corning Glass Works, Steuben Division
(Corning, N.Y.)
Glass, H 11 1/8 x Diam 4 3/4" (28.3 x 12.1 cm)
John C. Waddell Collection, Promised Gift of John C. Waddell
page 104

Centerpiece, 1932+
Manufacturer: Corning Glass Works, Steuben Division
(Corning, N.Y.)
Glass, H 3 x W 10 x D 10" (7.6 x 25.4 x 25.4 cm)
Collection of John C. Waddell
page 115

"Flying Buttresses" Textile, 1933
Manufacturer: Silks Beau Monde, Marshall Field and Company
(Chicago, Ill.)
Printed silk, L 15 x W 12" (38.1 x 30.5 cm)
John C. Waddell Collection, Gift of John C. Waddell, 1998
(1998.537.32)
page 74

"Bluebird" Radio, 1934
Manufacturer: Sparton Corporation (Jackson, Mich.)
Glass, chrome-plated metal, fabric, painted wood
H 14 1/4 x W 14 1/2 x D 7" (36.2 x 36.8 x 17.8 cm)
John C. Waddell Collection, Gift of John C. Waddell, 1998
(1998.537.31)
page 95

Vase, c. 1934
An example of this vase was shown in the 1934 "Machine Art"
exhibition at the Museum of Modern Art, New York
Manufacturer: Corning Glass Works, Steuben Division
(Corning, N.Y.)
Glass, H 8 3/4 x Diam 3 5/8" (22.2 x 9.2 cm)
John C. Waddell Collection, Promised Gift of John C. Waddell
page 112

"Bantam Special" Camera, 1936
Manufacturer: Eastman Kodak Company (Rochester, N.Y.)
Metal, enamel, H 3 1/2 x W 4 3/4 x D 1 3/4" (8.9 x 12.1 x 4.5 cm)
John C. Waddell Collection, Promised Gift of John C. Waddell
page 165

Desk Lamp, 1939
Manufacturer: Polaroid Corporation (Cambridge, Mass.)
Bakelite, aluminum
H 12 3/4 x W 11 1/2 x D 8 3/4" (32.4 x 29.2 x 22.2 cm)
John C. Waddell Collection, Promised Gift of John C. Waddell
page 162

WALTER DORWIN TEAGUE
EDWIN W. FUERST

"Embassy" Stemware, 1939
Designed for the State Dining Room, Federal Building,
New York World's Fair, 1939
Manufacturer: Libbey Glass Company (Toledo, Ohio)
Glass
Water glass: H 8 3/4 x Diam 2 3/4" (22.2 x 7 cm)
Parfait glass: H 8 1/8 x Diam 2 3/4" (20.6 x 7 cm)
Sherry glass: H 7 1/2 x Diam 2 3/4" (19.1 x 7 cm)
Burgundy glass: H 6 3/4 x Diam 2 3/4" (17.1 x 7 cm)
Claret glass: H 7 x Diam 2 3/4" (17.8 x 7 cm)
Cocktail glass: H 6 5/8 x Diam 2 7/8" (16.8 x 7.3 cm)
Champagne glass: H 6 5/8 x Diam 3 3/4" (16.8 x 9.5 cm)
Cordial glass: H 6 7/8 x Diam 2 3/4" (17.5 x 7 cm)
John C. Waddell Collection, Promised Gift of John C. Waddell
page 101

J. PALIN THORLEY
(American, born England, 1892–?)

Refrigerator Pitcher, 1940
Designed for the Westinghouse Electric Company
Manufacturer: The Hall China Company (East Liverpool, Ohio)
Earthenware, H 9 1/4 x W 3 1/2 x D 7 5/8" (19.4 x 9.0 x 23.5 cm)
Gift of David A. Hanks, 1981 (1981.445.9ab)
page 155

HAROLD L. VAN DOREN
(American, 1895–1957)
JOHN G. RIDEOUT
(American, 1898–1951)

"Sno-Plane" Sled, 1934
Manufacturer: The American National Company (Toledo, Ohio)
Painted wood, chrome-plated and painted metal
H 7 x W 25 x L 44" (17.8 x 63.5 x 111.8 cm)
Gift of Mark A. McDonald in memory of Ralph Cutler and
Mark Isaacson (1999.429)
page 132

JOHN VASSOS
(American, born Romania, 1898–1985)

"The Department Store," Illustration for Contempo
(by Ruth Vassos), 1929+
Publisher: E. P. Dutton & Company, Inc. (New York, N.Y.)
H 12 3/8 x W 9 3/8" (31.4 x 23.8 cm)
Collection of John C. Waddell
page 40

KURT VERSEN
(American, born Sweden, 1901–1997)

Table Lamp, c. 1935
Painted metal, cork
H 14 1/8 x W 11 1/8 x D 10 1/4" (35.9 x 28.3 x 26 cm)
John C. Waddell Collection, Gift of John C. Waddell, 1998
(1998.537.40)
page 161

WALTER VON NESSEN
(American, born Germany, 1889–1943)

Table Lamp, 1928
Manufacturer: Nessen Studio, Inc. (New York, N.Y.)
Silvered brass, H 31 x Diam 18 1/4" (78.7 x 46.4 cm)
John C. Waddell Collection, Gift of John C. Waddell, 1998
(1998.537.41a–d)
page 60

Floor Lamp, c. 1928
Manufacturer: Nessen Studio, Inc. (New York, N.Y.)
Chrome-plated brass, cast iron
H 67 3/4 x Diam 13 3/4" (172.1 x 34.9 cm)
John C. Waddell Collection, Promised Gift of John C. Waddell
page 61

Table, 1930
Manufacturer: Nessen Studio, Inc. (New York, N.Y.)
Aluminum, Bakelite
H 18 1/2 x W 15 1/4 x D 15 1/4" (47 x 38.7 x 38.7 cm)
Gifts in memory of Emil Blasberg, 1978 (1978.492.2)
page 91

"Diplomat" Coffee Service, 1933
Manufacturer: Chase Brass and Copper Company, Inc.
(Waterbury, Conn.)
Chrome-plated copper, composition
Coffee pot: H 8 1/2 x W 4 1/4 x D 6 5/8" (21.6 x 10.8 x 16.8 cm)
Sugar: H 2 7/8 x W 3 1/8 x D 2 1/2" (7.3 x 7.9 x 6.4 cm)
Creamer: H 4 1/2 x W 4 1/4 x D 5 1/2" (11.4 x 10.8 x 14 cm)
Tray: 1 1 1 1/8 x Diam 10 1/2" (2.9 x 26.7 cm)
John C. Waddell Collection, Promised Gift of John C. Waddell
page 43

"Continental" Coffee-Making Service, 1934
Exhibited in the 1934 exhibition "Contemporary American
Industrial Art" at The Metropolitan Museum of Art
Manufacturer: Chase Brass and Copper Company, Inc.
(Waterbury, Conn.)
Chrome-plated copper, composition
Coffee maker: H 10 1/8 x W 6 1/2 x D 4" (25.7 x 16.5 x 10.2 cm)
Sugar: H 3 3/4 x Diam 3" (9.5 x 7.6 cm)
Creamer: H 2 7/8 x W 5 x D 3" (7.3 x 12.7 x 7.6 cm)
John C. Waddell Collection, Promised Gift of John C. Waddell
pages 88–89

Design Drawings for "Continental" Coffee-Making Service, 1934
Manufacturer: Chase Brass and Copper Company, Inc.
(Waterbury, Conn.)
Pencil on paper, Framed: H 21 1/2 x W 32 1/8" (54.6 x 81.6 cm)
John C. Waddell Collection, Promised Gift of John C. Waddell
pages 88–89

SIDNEY BIEHLER WAUGH
(American, 1904–1963)

"Gazelle" Bowl, 1935
Manufacturer: Corning Glass Works, Steuben Division
(Corning, N.Y.)
Glass, H 7 1/4 x Diam 6 1/2" (18.4 x 16.5 cm)
Purchase, Edward C. Moore, Jr., Gift, 1935 (35.94.1ab)
page 41

KARL EMANUEL MARTIN
(KEM) WEBER
(American, born Germany, 1889–1963)

"Today" Vase, 1927
Manufacturer: Friedman Silver Company (New York, N.Y.)
Silver-plated metal, H 13 1/4 x Diam 3 5/8" (33.7 x 9.2 cm)
John C. Waddell Collection, Promised Gift of John C. Waddell
page 50

"Today" Cocktail Shaker, c. 1928
Manufacturer: Friedman Silver Company (New York, N.Y.)
Silver-plated metal, rosewood
H 10 7/8 x W 7 5/8 x D 4 3/4" (27.6 x 19.4 x 12.1 cm)
John C. Waddell Collection, Promised Gift of John C. Waddell
page 87

(Attributed)
"Zephyr" Electric Clock, c. 1934
Manufacturer: Lawson Time Inc. (Pasadena, Calif.)
Brass, Bakelite, H 3 1/4 x W 8 x D 3 1/8" (8.3 x 20.3 x 7.9 cm)
Gift of David A. Hanks, 1986 (1986.418.2)
page 136

"Airline" Armchair, c. 1934
Manufacturer: Airline Chair Company (Los Angeles, Calif.)
Wood, Naugahyde
H 31 1/2 x W 24 3/4 x D 33" (80 x 62.9 x 83.8 cm)
John C. Waddell Collection, Promised Gift of John C. Waddell
page 138

WILLIAM ARCHIBALD WELDEN
(American, 1892–1970)

"Empire" Cocktail Shaker, 1938
Manufacturer: Revere Copper and Brass Company (Rome, N.Y.)
Chrome-plated brass, Bakelite
H 12 1/8 x W 7 1/8 x D 3" (30.8 x 18.1 x 7.6 cm)
John C. Waddell Collection, Promised Gift of John C. Waddell
page 108

FRANK LLOYD WRIGHT
(American, 1867–1959)

Desk and Chair, c. 1936+
Made for the S. C. Johnson and Son Administration Building,
Racine, Wisconsin
Manufacturer: Steelcase, Inc. (Grand Rapids, Mich.)
Painted steel, walnut, brass
Desk: H 33 3/4 x W 84 x D 32" (85.7 x 213.4 x 81.3 cm)
Chair: H 36 x W 17 3/4 x D 20" (91.4 x 45.1 x 50.8 cm)
Lent by S. C. Johnson and Son, Inc.
page 160

RUSSEL WRIGHT
(American, 1904–1976)

Flatware, c. 1930
Silver, stainless steel
Butter knife: L 6 1/2" (16.5 cm)
Dinner knife: L 8 1/8" (20.6 cm)
Dinner fork: L 7 1/2" (19.1 cm)
Salad fork: L 6" (15.2 cm)
Soup spoon: L 5 1/8" (13 cm)
Teaspoon: L 6 5/8" (16.8 cm)
Gift of Russel Wright, 1976 (1976.67.52ab–54ab)
page 97

Salt and Pepper Shakers, c. 1930
Silver, Each: H 1 3/8 x W 1 1/8 x D 1 1/8" (3.5 x 2.9 x 2.9 cm)
Gift of Russel Wright, 1976 (1976.67.55, .56)
page 118

Cocktail Shaker and Two Goblets, c. 1931
Manufacturer: Russel Wright, Inc. (New York, N.Y.)
Pewter
Shaker: H 9 x W 4 3/4" (22.9 x 12.1 cm)
Goblets (each): H 2 1/2 x Diam 2 5/8" (6.4 x 6.7 cm)
John C. Waddell Collection, Promised Gift of John C. Waddell
page 120

Planter, c. 1932
Spun aluminum, H 5 1/2 x Diam 6 7/8" (14 x 17.5 cm)
John C. Waddell Collection, Promised Gift of John C. Waddell
page 111

Cocktail Shaker, c. 1932
Spun aluminum, cork, H 13 1/2 x Diam 3 7/8" (34.3 x 9.8 cm)
John C. Waddell Collection, Promised Gift of John C. Waddell
page 111

Spherical Vase, c. 1932
Spun aluminum, H 8 7/8 x Diam 10 1/8" (22.5 x 25.7 cm)
John C. Waddell Collection, Promised Gift of John C. Waddell
page 111

Pitcher, c. 1932
Spun aluminum, wood
H 10 1/8 x W 11 x D 6" (25.7 x 27.9 x 15.2 cm)
John C. Waddell Collection, Promised Gift of John C. Waddell
page 109

Salad-Serving Utensils, c. 1935
Chrome-plated metal, glass
Spoon: L 13 1/2" (34.3 cm)
Fork: L 12 7/8" (32.7 cm)
John C. Waddell Collection, Gift of John C. Waddell, 1998
(1998.537.43, .44)
page 96

"American Modern" Dinnerware, 1937
Manufacturer: Steubenville Pottery (East Liverpool, Ohio)
Earthenware
Pitcher: H 10 5/8 x W 8 1/2 x D 6 5/8" (27 x 21.6 x 16.8 cm)
Coffee pot: H 6 3/4 x W 8 1/4 x D 6" (17.1 x 21 x 15.2 cm)
Teapot: H 4 7/8 x W 10 x D 6 3/4" (12.4 x 25.4 x 17.1 cm)
Celery dish: H 1 1/4 x W 13 1/4 x D 3 5/8" (3.2 x 33.7 x 9.2 cm)
Gravy bowl: H 2 1/2 x W 9 x D 6 1/2" (6.4 x 22.9 x 16.5 cm)
Gravy underplate: H 1 x W 10 7/8 x D 6 1/4" (2.5 x 27.6 x 15.9 cm)
Salt and pepper shakers (each): H 2 1/8 x Diam 2 1/8"
(5.4 x 5.4 cm)
John C. Waddell Collection, Promised Gift of John C. Waddell
page 158

EVA ZEISEL
(American, born Hungary, 1906)
and students in the Industrial Design Department, Pratt Institute
(Brooklyn, N.Y.)

"Stratoware" Dinnerware, 1940
Manufacturer: Universal Potteries Inc. (Cambridge, Ohio)
Earthenware
Covered pitcher: H 8 1/4 x W 5 1/2 x D 3 1/4" (21 x 14 x 8.3 cm)
Creamer: H 4 3/4 x W 3 3/4 x D 2 3/8" (12.1 x 9.5 x 6 cm)
Sugar bowl: H 5 x W 4 1/4 x D 2 3/4" (12.7 x 10.8 x 7 cm)
Salt and pepper shakers (each): H 3 7/8 x W 2 1/4 x D 1 5/8"
(9.8 x 5.7 x 4.1 cm)
Teacups (each): H 2 1/8 x W 4 x D 5 1/8" (5.4 x 10.2 x 13 cm)
Saucers (each): Diam 6 3/8" (16.2 cm)
Dinner plate: Diam 9 5/8" (24.4 cm)
Bread plate: Diam 6 3/4" (17.1 cm)
Bowl: Diam 6 3/4" (17.1 cm)
John C. Waddell Collection, Promised Gift of John C. Waddell
page 159

DESIGNERS UNKNOWN

Armoire, c. 1926
Exhibited in 1926 in the fifth annual Arts in Trades
Club exhibition of decorative art, The Hotel Waldorf-Astoria,
New York, N.Y.
Manufacturer: The Company of Master Craftsmen for
W & J. Sloane (New York, N.Y.)
Thuyawood, mahogany, satinwood, plastic, ebony
H 53 x W 35 3/4 x D 20" (134.6 x 88.9 x 50.8 cm)
Purchase, Theodore R. Gamble Jr. Gift, in honor of his mother,
Mrs. Theodore Robert Gamble, 1980 (1980.333)
page 41

The Little Review, May 1929+
Printed paper, H 9 3/4 x W 7 3/4" (24.8 x 19.7 cm)
Collection of John C. Waddell
page 67

Table Lamp, c. 1935
Manufacturer: Pattyn Products Company (Detroit, Mich.)
Aluminum, Bakelite, glass, H 19 3/4 x Diam 8" (50.2 x 20.3 cm)
John C. Waddell Collection, Gift of John C. Waddell, 1998
(1998.537.42)
page 125

"TF-360" Theater Lighting Fixture, c. 1935
Manufacturer: Rambusch Decorating Company (New York, N.Y.)
Bronze, H 10 x W 8 7/8 x D 10 3/8" (25.4 x 22.5 x 26.4 cm)
Gift of The Rambusch Company, 1999 (1999.130.1)
page 144

Design Drawing for a "TF-360" Theater Lighting Fixture, c. 1935
Pencil on paper, H 18 x W 30" (45.7 x 76.2 cm)
Gift of The Rambusch Company, 1999 (1999.130.2)
page 144

Ice Gun, c. 1935
Manufacturer: Opco Company (Los Angeles, Calif.)
Enameled and chrome-plated steel
H 6 1/2 x W 11 x D 2 3/4" (16.5 x 27.9 x 7 cm)
John C. Waddell Collection, Promised Gift of Mark A.
McDonald
page 135

Low Table, c. 1937
Plate glass, H 16 1/4 x Diam 36" (41.3 x 91.4 cm)
Gift of Mr. and Mrs. Victor Gaines, 1976 (1976.417)
page 94

"Down Beat" Textile, c. 1940
Manufacturer: Scalamandré Silks (New York, N.Y.)
Silk, cotton, L 93 x W 50 1/2" (236.2 x 128.3 cm)
Gift of Franco Scalamandré, 1941 (41.28.1)
page 77

Biographies

EGMONT ARENS

b. Cleveland, Ohio 1888–d. New York, New York 1966
Arens spent his youth in New Mexico. In 1917 he moved to New York, where he founded the Flying Star Press. He served as art editor of *Vanity Fair* (1922–23) and managing editor of *Creative Arts Magazine* (1925–27). In 1929 he began his career as an industrial designer by establishing the industrial styling division of the Calkins and Holden Advertising Agency, where he stayed until 1935, the year he founded his own firm.

During the 1930s Arens wrote influential articles about "appetite appeal" for package design, in which, for example, he redesigned the container of a corn product (probably cereal) by replacing the image of an Indian maiden with that of an invitingly edible ear of corn. He also wrote critical articles about the deplorable quality of train and automobile design. Among his own product redesigns were the Parliament and Philip Morris cigarette packs and new packaging for the Great Atlantic & Pacific Tea Company. His industrial designs included the "Streamliner" meat slicer for Hobart Manufacturing Company and the Kitchen Aid mixer.

RALPH BARTON

b. Kansas City, Missouri 1891–d. New York, New York 1931
An artist and cartoonist whose satirical caricatures appeared in *Life, Vanity Fair, The New Yorker, Judge, Harper's Bazaar,* and *Liberty,* Barton illustrated Anita Loos's *Gentlemen Prefer Blondes* and a special edition of Balzac's *Droll Stories.* In 1924 he published a book titled *Science in Rhyme Without Reason.* Barton lived and worked in Europe for a time and returned to the United States in 1929. Picking up on the *Gentlemen Prefer Blondes* theme, Stehli Silks Corporation commissioned him to produce designs for its "Americana" series of textiles in 1927.

LESTER BEALL

b. Kansas City, Missouri 1903–d. Brookfield, Connecticut 1969
A graphic designer influenced by the Bauhaus school and Russian constructivist art, Beall set up a studio in Chicago in 1926. His work ranged from murals and posters to logotypes and typography. Among Beall's clients during the 1930s were the Public Service Company of Northern Illinois, *The Chicago Tribune,* the R. R. Donnelly Corporation, the Rural Electrification Administration, CBS, RCA, Time Inc., Hiram Walker, and the Upjohn Company. In 1935 Beall moved to New York, where he was hired to design *The New Republic* magazine and twenty McGraw-Hill publications.

NORMAN BEL GEDDES

b. Adrian, Michigan 1893–d. New York, New York 1958
From 1916 to 1927, Bel Geddes designed productions for theater, operas, and Hollywood films. He collaborated with Frank Lloyd Wright on Aline Barnsdall's theater project in Los Angeles and maintained a friendship with the Expressionist architect Erich Mendelsohn, whose influence Bel Geddes credited for his decision to enter the industrial design field. In 1927 he opened his own office. Many of his clients came through the J. Walter Thompson advertising agency, for which he served as a consultant; he also redesigned the company's headquarters. Bel Geddes's work included furniture, accessories, and household products such as radios and syphon bottles. His visionary designs for transportation included a torpedo-shaped ocean liner, streamlined automobiles for Chrysler and Plymouth, and airplanes. He designed the Futurama Pavilion for General Motors at the 1939 New York World's Fair and published his theories of design and urban planning in *Horizons* (1932) and *Magic Motorways* (1940).

THEODORE C. BROOKHART

dates unknown
Little is known about Brookhart, who, with Egmont Arens, designed the "Streamliner" meat slicer for Hobart Manufacturing Company (Troy, Ohio).

FREDERICK CARDER

b. Staffordshire, England 1863–d. Corning, New York 1963
In 1903 the forty-year-old Carder, a successful English glassmaker, was hired to enlarge the production capabilities of the H. W. Hawkes Glass factory in Corning, New York. Within a year, Hawkes and Carder renamed the firm the Steuben Glass Company. Carder went on to develop new technology as well as new types of glass. Especially successful was "Aurene," an iridescent glass that competed with Tiffany's "Favrile" glass. Between 1903 and 1932 Carder designed more than seven thousand varieties of decorative and useful objects. Most of Steuben's output was sold by traveling representatives to department stores such as B. Altman's, New York; Marshall Field's, Chicago; and Gump's, San Francisco. In 1918 Steuben was taken over by the Corning Glass Works, a producer of commercial glassware. Carder remained art director of the Steuben Division until 1932, after which he pursued his career in art-glass production.

F. V. CARPENTER

dates unknown
Carpenter was an illustrator whose drawings and sketches of New York City appeared in the periodical *Pencil Points* in the late 1920s and 1930s. He was commissioned by the Stehli Silks Corporation to produce a design for its "Americana" series of textiles in 1927.

DONALD DESKEY

b. Blue Earth, Minnesota 1894–d. Vero Beach, Florida 1989
Deskey began working as a designer in the late 1920s after briefly pursuing a career as an artist and in advertising. In 1926 he returned to the United States from Europe, where he had studied painting, traveled to the Bauhaus, and visited the 1925 Exposition des Arts Décoratifs et Industriels Modernes in Paris. That same year he created modern window settings for the fashionable New York department stores Saks Fifth Avenue and Franklin Simon, experimenting with new industrial materials such as cork, Transite (a high-density fiber cement board), and chrome-plated metals. By 1927 Deskey formed a design partnership with Phillip Vollmer and began to make furniture, lighting, and screens. At first, this inventive, Bauhaus-inspired furniture of undecorated metal and Bakelite was custom-made. In the

1930s, however, many of Deskey's designs were mass-produced. He won the competition to design the interiors for Radio City Music Hall, which were completed in 1932. He was one of the founding members of the American Designers Gallery Inc., in New York, participating in its inaugural exhibition of 1928. Deskey's work was included in the era's most important exhibitions of contemporary industrial design, including "Modern American Design in Metal" at the Newark Museum (1929) and "Contemporary American Industrial Art, 1934, Thirteenth Exhibition" and "Contemporary American Industrial Art, 1940: Fifteenth Exhibition" at The Metropolitan Museum of Art.

HENRY DREYFUSS
b. New York, New York 1904–d. South Pasadena, California 1972

In 1929, after an early career as a stage designer working for Norman Bel Geddes, Dreyfuss turned to industrial design and founded his own firm. He set himself apart from his peers by doing pioneering work in the field of ergonomics and by stressing safety and utility while still creating stylish streamlined objects for prestigious clients. Dreyfuss's now iconic designs included a new design for the "20th Century Limited" railroad train, the "Model 300" and "Trimline" telephones for Bell Telephone Laboratories, and insulated carafes for the American Thermos Company. By the mid-1950s Dreyfuss maintained offices on both the east and west coasts. In 1969 he retired from his firm, which continues today under his name.

HELEN DRYDEN
b. Baltimore, Maryland 1887–d. 1934

Dryden was a successful fashion illustrator, designing at least ninety-one covers for *Vogue* between 1910 and 1923. She was commissioned by the Stehli Silks Corporation to produce designs for its "Americana" series of textiles in 1927. In 1928 she turned to industrial design. Dryden created two modern pianos for an American manufacturer, and in 1938 she collaborated with Raymond Loewy on the Studebaker automobile.

HELEN A. HUGHES DULANY
b. 1895–d. Los Angeles, California 1991

Active in Chicago from 1931 to 1936, Dulany was a designer of metal tableware and glass. She also collaborated with the glass designer Maurice Heaton.

WILLIAM ADDISON DWIGGINS
b. Martinsville, Ohio 1880–d. Hingham, Massachusetts 1956

Dwiggins, a Boston-based graphic artist, designed typefaces, layouts, and modern graphics for numerous publications in the 1920s and 1930s. During his early career he designed commercial advertisements but always preferred book design to all other work. He produced more than three hundred designs for the publisher Alfred A. Knopf, and in 1931 he designed H. G. Wells's *The Time Machine*, published by Random House. His work appeared on the cover of The Metropolitan Museum of Art's 1929 catalogue for "The Architect and the Industrial Arts" exhibition.

CHARLES BUCKLES FALLS
b. Fort Wayne, Indiana 1874–d. New York, New York 1960

Falls, a prominent printmaker, was also a designer of stage sets and costumes, a magazine illustrator, and a noted mural painter. He was active in various arts societies and a member of several clubs, including the New York Architectural League and the Philadelphia Sketch Club. Falls was commissioned by the Stehli Silks Corporation to produce designs for its "Americana" series of textiles in 1927.

ROBERT FAWCETT
b. London, England 1903–d. Ridgefield, Connecticut 1967

Fawcett's family left London for Canada and then moved to New York, where Fawcett pursued a career in commercial art until enrolling at the Slade Art School in London. After his return to New York, he became a popular illustrator. He was commissioned to design the cover of Theodore Dreiser's book, *Epitaph, 1929*.

HUGH FERRISS
b. St. Louis, Missouri 1889–d. New York, New York 1962

An architect, draftsman, and theorist, Ferriss moved to New York from St. Louis in 1912 to work as a draftsman in the office of architect Cass Gilbert. In 1915 Ferriss left Gilbert's employ and became a freelance illustrator and delineator (architectural renderer). By the early 1920s he was producing finished perspective drawings, particularly of skyscrapers and other commercial architecture. Ferriss published his best-known book, *The Metropolis of Tomorrow*, in 1929, and his stature in the architectural establishment grew steadily thereafter. Although he was a licensed architect, Ferriss elected to build on paper only, never erecting a structure.

PAUL T. FRANKL
b. Vienna, Austria 1887–d. New York, New York 1958

After training as an architect in Vienna and Berlin, Frankl emigrated to the United States in 1914. He became one of the most important promoters of the modern style in America through his publications as well as his designs. He opened his own gallery/showroom on Madison Avenue in 1924, selling both his own work and European imports. As early as 1925 he made geometric cabinets, desks, and bookcases in an architectural manner, which he titled "Skyscraper" furniture for its resemblance to the angled and stepped high-rise buildings of New York City. Frankl showed an entire room at the 1928 "Art in Trade" exhibition at Macy's. Devoted to the cause of modern decorative arts, he wrote the influential books *New Dimensions* (1928) and *Form and Re-Form* (1930). Frankl also helped establish the American Designers Gallery and the American Union of Decorative Artists and Craftsmen.

EDWIN W. FUERST
b. 1903–d. Franklin, Massachussetts 1988

In 1936 the Owens-Illinois Glass Company hired Fuerst to design its "Modern American" line in an attempt to recapture its earlier success as a manufacturer of commercial glass products. The line was first produced in 1939 for private clients and in 1940 was made available to the general public. It was discontinued in the early 1940s when the company concentrated on production for wartime use.

PAOLO GARRETTO
b. Naples, Italy 1903–d. Monaco 1989

Garretto was a graphic artist whose illustrations appeared in such European periodicals as *Gebrauchsgraphik* and *Arts et Metiers Graphiques*. In the United States, *Fortune*, the American business and industry magazine, commissioned Garretto for the cover of its August 1932 issue.

KNEELAND L. ("RUZZIE") GREEN
b. 1892–d. 1956

Green became a director of the Stehli Silks Corporation soon after joining the company as a stylist in January 1925. He was selected by the Silk Association of America to represent the industry as a member of the U.S. Commission to the 1925 Paris Exposition. Green designed textiles for the "Americana" series by Stehli Silks.

LURELLE GUILD
b. New York, New York 1898–d. Darien, Connecticut 1985

Guild began his career when he was hired to illustrate interiors for *House & Garden* in the early 1920s. He and his wife collaborated for seven years in a successful illustration career until they realized many of their designs were being put into production by manufacturers of products such as linoleum, furniture, and textiles. Guild left illustration for industrial design, and in 1930 produced the "Model 30" vacuum cleaner for Electrolux. His client list included companies as wide-ranging as Carrier Engineering Corporation for air-conditioning units, General Electric, Columbia Mills, the New Haven Railroad, the Chase Brass & Copper Company, the Aluminum Company of America, and International Silver.

REUBEN HALEY

b. Pittsburgh, Pennsylvania 1872–d. Beaver, Pennsylvania 1933

Haley specialized in glass design, working for a number of American manufacturers. He also made designs for metal and ceramic wares, including a line of art pottery for the Muncie Pottery Company of Indiana. From 1911 to 1925 he worked for U.S. Glass, where he rose to the position of chief designer. In 1925 he opened the Metal Products Company in space rented from Consolidated Lamp & Glass Company in Coraopolis, Pennsylvania. Haley created a line of glassware known as the "Ruba Rombic" pattern, "so ultra-smart that it is as new as tomorrow's newspaper" (Shirley Paine in *Garden and Home Builder*, July 1928).

JOHN HELD, JR.

b. Salt Lake City, Utah 1889–d. Belmar, New Jersey 1958
Held, who studied with the painter and sculptor Mahonri Mackintosh Young, settled in New York in 1912. He became a popular cartoonist whose drawings, which epitomized the 1920s Jazz Age, were illustrated in *The New Yorker*, *Cosmopolitan*, *Vanity Fair*, and *Life*. He was commissioned by the Stehli Silks Corporation to produce designs for the "Americana" series of textiles in 1927.

WOLFGANG HOFFMANN

b. Vienna, Austria 1900–d. Chicago, Illinois 1969

POLA HOFFMANN

b. Stryz, Poland, 1902–d. ?
Wolgang Hoffmann was the son of architect and designer Josef Hoffmann, one of the founders of the Wiener Werkstätte. After studying in Vienna and working in his father's office, he immigrated to New York in 1925 with his wife, Pola, a fellow student at the Kunstgewerbeschule. In 1926 he opened his own studio, making metal furniture, lighting fixtures, pewterware, and textiles. As a member of the American Union of Decorative Artists and Craftsmen, he and Kem Weber organized a major exhibition of contemporary design at the Brooklyn Museum of Art in 1931, the same year that his metalwork was exhibited at The Metropolitan Museum of Art. Pola was known primarily as a textile designer but collaborated with Wolfgang on metal table accessories. The Hoffmanns divorced in the 1930s and dissolved their business partnership as well.

FRANK G. HOLMES

b. Pawtucket, Rhode Island 1878–d. New York, New York 1954
Unlike most designers of the period, Holmes began his career by studying at a design college, the Rhode Island School of Design. Between 1898 and 1901 he designed silver for the Howard Sterling Company in Providence. He then moved to New York, and in 1905 he began an almost fifty-year career as designer for Lenox Inc., manufacturer of china tableware. He designed china for presidents Warren Harding, Franklin Roosevelt, and Harry Truman and was appointed by Herbert Hoover as a member of the American commission to report on the 1925 Exposition des Arts Décoratifs et Industriels Modernes in Paris.

ILONKA KARASZ

b. Budapest, Hungary 1896–d. New York, New York 1981
After immigrating to the United States in 1913, Karasz created the first modern advertisements for the retailers Bonwit Teller, Ovington's, and others. A versatile artist, she soon added textile and wallpaper design as well as ceramics, silver, furniture, and book illustration to her oeuvre. Karasz's early style had a naïve, handcrafted look, but it came to be characterized by much sleeker, abstract patterning. By 1928 Karasz exhibited her work at the American Designers Gallery. She was member of the American Union of Decorative Artists and Craftsmen, and, in 1931, Kem Weber chose her textile designs to accompany his installation.

CLARENCE KARSTADT

b. 1902–d. Santa Monica, California 1968
Little is known about Karstadt, who designed the "Silvertone" radio (Model 6110) in 1938 for Sears, Roebuck and Company, Chicago.

CLAYTON KNIGHT

b. Rochester, New York 1891–d. Redding, Connecticut 1969
Knight studied art under George Bellows and Robert Henri. In 1912, he became an instructor at the Art Institute of Chicago. He was commissioned by the Stehli Silks Corporation to design textiles for its "Americana" series in 1927.

WILLIAM LESCAZE

b. Geneva, Switzerland 1896–d. New York, New York 1969
In 1920 Lescaze, who trained as an architect, moved from Switzerland to Cleveland, Ohio, to work for the firms of Hubbell and Benes and Walter McCormack. In 1923 he established his own practice in New York, taking on commissions to design several apartments, a boys' dormitory for a private school in Greenwich, Connecticut (1925), and the Capital Bus Terminal in New York (1927). In 1929 he formed a partnership with George Howe, a well-established Philadelphia architect. It was during this period that Howe and Lescaze designed the thirty-three-story skyscraper for the Philadelphia Saving Fund Society (1929–33), which became an icon of modern architecture.

After the partnership dissolved in 1938, Lescaze maintained his architecture practice and continued to design furniture, lighting, clocks, and silver accessories. He produced a metal cantilevered chair, upholstered seating, a microphone, and a mobile truck unit for CBS, whose Hollywood studios he designed in 1938. Among the many exhibitions in which Lescaze took part were the 1927 "Machine-Age Exposition" in New York, Macy's 1928 "International Exhibition of Modern Interiors," the New York World's Fair of 1939, and the 1934 "Contemporary American Industrial Art" exhibition at The Metropolitan Museum of Art.

PAUL LOBEL

b. Romania, 1899–d. New York, New York 1983
In 1924 and 1925, Lobel studied at the Art Students League in New York. He attended the 1925 Exposition des Arts Décoratifs et Industriels Modernes in Paris, finding inspiration in the design of three-dimensional objects. Upon returning to New York, Lobel designed two metal fireplaces and a number of accessories for Eugene Schoen. He participated in Macy's "Art in Trade" show (1928) and The Metropolitan Museum of Art's "The Architect and the Industrial Arts" exhibition (1929). In 1929 Lobel organized the firm of Lobel-Uris with Leo J. Uris and began experimenting with a process for bending glass. He produced a wide variety of objects using this "Benduro" process. Lobel also worked in other materials, producing lamps for American Designs, Inc.; screens, tables, trays, and other accessories in wood for Broadweve Furniture Company; and commercial interiors of fabricated metal. He, along with Eliel Saarinen, designed tea and coffee services for the 1934 exhibition "Contemporary American Industrial Art" at The Metropolitan Museum of Art.

RAYMOND LOEWY

b. Paris, France 1893–d. Monte Carlo, Monaco 1986
In 1919, Loewy moved to New York from Paris to pursue a career as a commercial artist and fashion illustrator. However, his knowledge of electrical engineering and his fascination with steam locomotives and all modes of modern transportation propelled him to open an industrial design firm in 1929. He modernized the duplicating machine for Gestetner Duplicating Company, creating a sleek, stylish housing of molded plastic. This project, of 1929, was followed by highly visible successes such as the Hupmobile automobile (1934), the ColdSpot refrigerator (1934), the streamlined S-1 locomotive for the Pennsylvania Railroad (1937), and the well-known Studebaker "Champion" (1947) and "Avanti" (1962) automobiles. Loewy was a master at corporate identity and package design. Among his clients were Lucky Strike Cigarette Company, Coca-Cola, Pepsodent, and the National Biscuit Company. In later years he worked for NASA, designing the interior of Skylab.

LOUIS LOZOWICK

b. Ludvinovka, Ukraine 1892–d. South Orange, New Jersey 1973

After emigrating from the Ukraine in 1906, Lozowick attended art school and graduated from Ohio State University. He settled in New York in 1924 and began painting as well as making lithographs, many of which were based on the architecture of the city. His "Machine Ornament" series of ink drawings was exhibited at J. B. Neumann's New Art Circle in 1926, and he exhibited in, as well as assisted in the organization of, the 1927 "Machine-Age Exposition" in New York. Lozowick continued to show his paintings, drawings, and lithographs until his death in 1973.

JOHN R. MORGAN

dates unknown

In addition to the "Waterwitch" outboard motor, which he designed for Sears, Roebuck and Company in 1936, Morgan's other designs included roller skates and radios (sold under the "Silvertone" label). His designs were illustrated by Harold Van Doren in his 1940 book *Industrial Design: A Practical Guide.*

PETER MÜLLER-MUNK

b. Berlin, Germany 1904–d. Pittsburgh, Pennsylvania 1967

Müller-Munk is best known for his 1935 design of a chrome-plated brass pitcher called the "Normandie" for its resemblance to the sleek silhouette of the French ocean liner's prow. He moved to New York in 1926 after studying design with Bruno Paul and silversmithing with Waldenar Ramisch in Berlin. After a year designing for Tiffany, he set up his own workshop. Müller-Munk's products were shown at all of the important design exhibitions of the 1920s and 1930s. By the mid-1930s he incorporated new materials in his wide repertoire, which included the Waring Blender and products for Westinghouse, Texaco, and U.S. Steel. Peter Müller-Munk Associates remains located in Pittsburgh.

ISAMU NOGUCHI

b. Los Angeles, California 1904–d. New York, New York 1988

Noguchi, born to an American mother and a Japanese father, was raised in Japan and trained there as a cabinetmaker. In 1918 he was sent to America where he became increasingly committed to sculpture. After studying under Constantin Brancusi in Paris, Noguchi returned to the United States in 1932. He lived mainly in New York where he maintained a studio and designed theater sets, as well as costumes and ballet sets for Martha Graham. In 1937 he designed his first industrial product, "Radio Nurse," a helmetlike Bakelite device for listening in to sounds in other rooms of a house. Noguchi continued his career as a sculptor while designing furniture for Herman Miller and Knoll, glass for Steuben, and lighting with paper shades under his own label, Akari.

WILBER L. ORME

b. Cambridge, Ohio 1889–d. Shagrin Falls, Ohio 1972

Orme designed the "Pristine Table Architecture" series for Cambridge Glass Company of Cambridge, Ohio, in 1938. Part of the National Glass Company consortium from 1901 to 1907, Cambridge produced high-end glassware in the 1920s and 1930s.

PETER PFISTERER

b. Basel, Switzerland 1907

In 1934 Pfisterer, a designer of lighting and home furnishings, collaborated with Richard Neutra on a housing model, "One-Plus-Two," which was designed to permit three separate successive stages of building to accommodate an expanding family. Pfisterer's contribution to the project included indirect illumination from ceiling reflectors that would receive the light from vacuum tubes under the exterior roof projections. In 1940 he won the Museum of Modern Art competition for home-furnishing designs for his movable lighting equipment.

RUTH REEVES

b. Redlands, California 1892–d. New York, New York 1966

In 1920 Reeves went to Paris to work under Fernand Léger, having studied painting in New York and San Francisco. Upon her return to the United States in 1927, she began a successful career as a textile designer. She was a founding member of the American Designers Gallery in New York, where she exhibited in 1928 and 1929. In 1930 W. & J. Sloane commissioned a series of contemporary textiles for home furnishings, which were shown later that year at The Metropolitan Museum of Art exhibition "Decorative Metal Work and Cotton Textiles." Reeves's designs ranged from the abstract to more realistic scenes of contemporary life and reflected her interest in the urban landscape of soaring skyscrapers, expansion bridges, and sophisticated citizens. In 1932 she created a wall tapestry and rug for the Grand Foyer of Radio City Music Hall.

LOUIS W. RICE

dates unknown

Rice, who was active from 1899 as a silversmith in New York, became president of Bernard Rice's Sons around 1917. His "Skyscraper" tableware designs of 1928 were manufactured by Bernard Rice's Sons, Inc., as part of their "Apollo Studios" line.

JOHN GORDON RIDEOUT

b. St. Paul, Minnesota 1898–d. Cleveland, Ohio 1951

Codesigner, with Harold Van Doren, of the "Sno-Plane" sled, Rideout also designed one of the first plastic radio cabinets for Air-King Products Company in 1933. Rideout was one of the organizers of the Society of Industrial Designers of New York.

GILBERT ROHDE

b. New York, New York 1894–d. New York, New York 1944

The son of a New York cabinetmaker, Rohde began as a political cartoonist and furniture illustrator. In 1927, after returning from a trip to France, he turned to custom furniture design, interpreting the modern French style he had just seen. By 1929 he opened his own studio and began to produce designs for Haywood-Wakefield, Troy Sunshade, John Widdecomb, Thonet, and Herman Miller. His progressive furniture incorporated materials such as chrome and Bakelite, and he was one of the first to bring modern designs—including modular furniture and sectional sofas—to mass production. Rohde produced a series of clocks for the Herman Miller Clock Company and designed interiors for private clients and public spaces. His interiors were shown at the "Design for Living" house at the 1933 Century of Progress exhibition in Chicago, The Metropolitan Museum of Art's 1934 "Contemporary American Industrial Art" exhibition, Macy's and Wanamaker's department stores, the Museum of Modern Art's "Machine Art" exhibition of 1934, and the New York World's Fair of 1939.

HERMAN ROSSE

b. The Hague, Netherlands 1887–d. Nyack, New York 1965

From 1907 until 1909 Rosse worked in the London office of the noted Arts and Crafts architect C. F. A. Voysey. In 1909 he moved to the United States. He received his first major commission in 1911, designing interiors for the Peace Palace in The Hague. Later Rosse was responsible for interior designs at the Dutch pavilions at the 1915 Panama-Pacific International Exposition in San Francisco, the 1936 World's Fair in Brussels, and the 1939 New York World's Fair. From 1915 until his death, he designed sets and costumes for hundreds of stage and motion-picture productions, winning an Academy Award for his art direction of the film *King of Jazz,* released in 1930. In 1928 he became the founding president of the American Designers Gallery. He went back to Holland in 1933 and did not return to the United States until 1947. In the United States, he continued designing for the theater until his death in 1965.

ELIEL SAARINEN

b. Rantasalmi, Finland 1873–d. Bloomfield Hills, Michigan 1950

Saarinen formed his first architectural partnership in Finland in 1896. With his two partners he designed the Finnish Pavilion at the 1900 Paris Exposition. The partnership dissolved in 1907, and Saarinen continued on his own to design buildings and furniture. In 1912, Saarinen designed the Helsinki Railway Station, which brought him international recognition. He participated in European exhibitions such as the Salon d'Automme in Paris

1907 and the Cologne Deutscher Werkbund exhibition in 1914. Saarinen moved to the United States after winning second prize in the 1922 Chicago Tribune Tower competition. In 1925 he was asked to develop the Cranbrook Academy of Art in Bloomfield Hills, Michigan, and became president of the Academy in 1932. Saarinen's own house at Cranbrook included furniture, glass, silver, brass, and other furnishings of his own design. His wife Loja designed and executed rugs and textiles for the house and for other Cranbrook buildings. In 1929 Saarinen designed a dining room for The Metropolitan Museum of Art's exhibition "The Architect and the Industrial Arts," and in 1934 he showed a "Room for a Lady" at the museum's "Contemporary American Industrial Art" exhibition.

GEORGE SAKIER
b. Brooklyn, New York 1897–d. Paris, France 1988
Sakier attributed the First International Design Exhibition held in Munich as the inspiration for leaving his career as an art director (for French *Vogue, Harper's Bazaar,* and *Modes and Manners)* and turning to industrial design. Beginning in 1927 he developed designs for the American Radiator and Standard Sanitation Company, and in 1929 he designed functional modern objects such as bathroom fixtures and domestic glassware for Fostoria Glass Company. His first bathroom design was installed at the Waldorf-Astoria Hotel in 1931, and his first prefabricated bathroom was installed in 1933 in the 233 apartments of a Washington, D.C., building.

EUGENE SCHOEN
b. New York, New York 1880–d. New York, New York 1957
Schoen studied architecture at Columbia University and subsequently traveled to Vienna, where he continued his studies under Otto Wagner and Josef Hoffmann. He returned to New York and opened his own architectural practice in 1905. After visiting the 1925 Paris Exposition des Arts Décoratifs et Industriels Modernes, he added interior-design services to his firm. Schoen was commissioned for the interior designs of Rockefeller Center. He participated in Macy's 1928 exhibition "Art in Trade," as well as The Metropolitan Museum of Art's 1929 exhibition "The Architect and the Industrial Arts." In 1933 Schoen designed the Century of Progress in Chicago, and in 1934 he participated in the exhibition "Contemporary American Industrial Art" at The Metropolitan Museum of Art. He championed the use of innovative modern materials such as Fabrikoid, Flexwood, and Monel metal in both furniture and interiors and advocated a pale, monochromatic color scheme and indirect lighting in his interiors.

CHARLES SHEELER
b. Philadelphia, Pennsylvania 1883–d. Dobbs Ferry, New York 1965

A painter and photographer, Sheeler also maintained an interest in designing objects for the home that reflected the modern Bauhaus philosophy of "less is more." His abstracted designs of the 1920s and 1930s for tableware, glass, textiles, and furniture were simplified and streamlined into precise forms.

EDWARD J. STEICHEN
b. Luxembourg 1879–d. West Redding, Connecticut 1973
Steichen, who trained as a lithographer, began a career in photography in 1895 and in 1902 was a founding member of the Photo-Secession group. In 1925, the Stehli Silks Corporation commissioned him to produce photographs that were made into designs for its "Americana" series of textiles.

J. ROBERT F. SWANSON
b. Menominee, Michigan 1900–d. Birmingham, Michigan 1981
Having earned a B.A. in architecture from the University of Michigan in 1922, Swanson pursued graduate studies there under the Finnish architect Eliel Saarinen. In 1926 Swanson eloped with Saarinen's daughter, Eva Lisa (Pipsan). He began his own architectural firm and put his wife in charge of interior design. The Swansons collaborated on several projects, including metalwork for Cray of Boston, lamps for the Mutual-Sunset Lamp Manufacturing Company, printed fabrics for Goodall Fabrics, and glassware for U.S. Glass of Tiffin, Ohio. In 1929 they produced the "Flexible Home Arrangements" line of furniture for the Johnson Furniture Company of Grand Rapids, Michigan. In 1944 the Swansons formed a new partnership with Eliel Saarinen and his son Eero. The team completed projects such as the Des Moines Art Center, the Milwaukee Cultural Center, and Drake University in Des Moines. By 1947 the Swansons established Swanson Associates, and the firm began to take on commissions for churches, hospitals, banks, schools, and private institutions.

WALTER DORWIN TEAGUE
b. Decatur, Indiana 1883–d. Flemington, New Jersey 1960
Teague was among the first industrial designers in America and practiced as a freelance consultant. Before entering industrial design he achieved prominence as an advertising artist and as an authority on typography. In the 1930s financially hard-hit manufacturers were looking to the professional industrial designer for new products that would revive sagging business. Teague's first major client was Eastman Kodak, which had been given his name by Richard Bach, curator at The Metropolitan Museum of Art. Teague redesigned the company's showroom as well as its cameras, notably the famous "Baby Brownie" of molded plastic. In 1930 he designed an automobile for Marmon, and in 1932 Corning Glass gave Teague a one-year contract to prop up its diminishing returns. Teague produced a modern line of crystal tableware and shaped a new corporate image through a promo-

tional campaign. From 1933 to 1936 he created a line of streamlined blue-mirrored radios for the Sparton Radio Company. In 1944, along with Henry Dreyfuss and Raymond Loewy, he founded the American Society of Industrial Designers and was its first president. As chairman of the Board of Design, Teague took an active role in the 1939 New York World's Fair, and he personally designed the Ford Motor Company Building and the National Cash Register Building. His 1940 book, *Design This Day: The Technique of Order in the Machine Age,* espoused a "fundamental redesign of our world" in a modern functionalist manner that was influenced especially by Le Corbusier's emphasis on classic geometry and by the architecture of Walter Gropius and Robert Mallet-Stevens, which he had seen in Europe in 1926.

J. PALIN THORLEY
b. England 1892–d. ?
Thorley was taught to make pottery by his father. He completed a seven-year apprenticeship at the Wedgwood factory, where he worked after serving in World War I. In 1929 he came to the United States to work for various ceramic manufacturers. Thorley became art director of Hall China Company of East Liverpool, Ohio, and advised other local potteries on design for production.

HAROLD L. VAN DOREN
b. Chicago, Illinois 1895–d. Philadelphia, Pennsylvania 1957
In 1933 with John Gordon Rideout, Van Doren formed a design studio in Toledo, Ohio, where his first client was the Toledo Scale Company. Among his most important designs were the 1930–31 Air-King Products green plastic skyscraper radio, the "Mirror-Glo" gas heater marketed by the Utility Gas Appliance Company, and the streamlined "Sno-Plane" sled for American National Company. Van Doren worked for a number of companies during the 1930s, including Philco and Goodyear, and later for General Electric and Maytag. He was the author of *Industrial Design: A Practical Guide,* published in 1940.

JOHN VASSOS
b. Bucharest, Romania 1898–d. New York, New York 1985
Vassos immigrated to the United States in 1919, coming first to Boston and then settling in New York in 1924. He worked in advertising before turning to industrial design and illustration. In 1934 *Fortune* magazine claimed that Vassos's redesign of a New York City subway turnstile lowered production costs while increasing its sales. Among his other designs were a television console and the "RCA Victor Special" portable phonograph. His graphic illustrations included the cover of *Ultimo* and illustrations for *Contempo,* both books written by his wife, Ruth Vassos.

KURT VERSEN
b. Sweden 1901–d. Palm Beach, Florida 1997

In 1930 Versen settled in the United States and began working as a designer and manufacturer of lighting for commercial interiors and public buildings. As early as 1931 Howe and Lescaze commissioned him to produce the indirect lighting system for their modernist Philadelphia Saving Fund Society Building. Versen was later commissioned to design the lighting for the 1939 New York World's Fair, and throughout the 1940s and 1950s he manufactured a wide range of fixtures and flexible lamps than could be used for direct or indirect lighting.

WALTER VON NESSEN
b. Berlin, Germany 1889–d. Wiscasset, Maine 1943
MARGARETTA VON NESSEN
b. Sweden c. 1900–d. United States c. 1978

Walter Von Nessen studied under Bruno Paul at the Kunstgewerbeschule in Berlin, where he absorbed the philosophies of the Deutscher Werkbund and the Wiener Werkstätte. He worked on the redesign of the Berlin subway and designed furniture in Stockholm before moving to New York in 1923. Von Nessen met his future wife, Margaretta, while working in Sweden. She became his design collaborator. The Nessen Studio was established in 1927 to produce metal furniture and innovative lighting. The firm's 1928 standing floor lamp of brushed, chrome-plated brass and cast iron was used by Eliel Saarinen for the interiors of the Cranbrook Academy in Bloomfield Hills, Michigan.

SIDNEY BIEHLER WAUGH
b. Amherst, Massachusetts 1904–d. New York, New York 1963

Waugh began his artistic career as a sculptor, studying under Emile Bourdelle in Paris and winning a Prix de Rome in 1929. In 1932 he settled into a studio on Bleecker Street in New York, where he concentrated on architectural sculpture. He was hired by the Corning Glass Works in 1936 to reorganize its Steuben Division. He remained its chief designer until his death. Waugh used the innovative technology and new materials invented at Corning to design glass tableware in a modern aesthetic. His "lens" bowls were made of a refined form of the glass used for traffic lights and automobile headlights, and were cut in the same way. Waugh also produced contemporary designs to show off Steuben's composition of colorless crystal, a glass that provided an exceptional degree of transparency.

KARL EMANUEL MARTIN (KEM) WEBER
b. Berlin, Germany 1889–d. Santa Barbara, California 1963

Weber was apprenticed to the royal cabinetmaker in Potsdam and later studied under Bruno Paul in Berlin. He came to America just before World War I to assist in architectural work for the German section of the 1915 Panama-Pacific International Exposition in San Francisco. Stranded in the United States by the war, Weber settled in Los Angeles and by 1927 opened his own industrial design studio. He was among the leading contemporary designers to promote modernism on the West Coast, yet he maintained a strong presence in the East by exhibiting at Macy's exhibitions, at the American Union of Decorative Artists and Craftsmen, and at The Metropolitan Museum of Art. His early designs were influenced by the burgeoning International Style, but he later modified the hard edges of that aesthetic and embraced more streamlined, curvilinear form. Among Weber's designs were clocks for Lawson Time, tubular-steel and plywood furniture, and a prefabricated housing system for the Douglas Fir Plywood Association of Tacoma, Washington.

WILLIAM ARCHIBALD WELDEN
b. 1892–d. Sacramento, California 1970

Welden produced metalwork for architecture and lighting, as well as models for metal accessories by Norman Bel Geddes under his own manufacturer, Kantack. In the mid-1930s, he was hired as an independent designer for Revere Copper and Brass Company. Welden remained at Revere for the rest of his career, designing the now iconic "Revere Ware" line of copper-bottomed stainless steel pots and pans.

FRANK LLOYD WRIGHT
b. Richland Center, Wisconsin 1867–d. Phoenix, Arizona 1959

Wright's first architectural project was the design of his own house in 1889, while working as a draftsman for Adler & Sullivan of Chicago. He left Sullivan, who remained a life-long influence, in 1893 to become an independent architect. By 1900 Wright had designed more than fifty Prairie Style houses and had a highly successful career. That style expressed his philosophy of organic architecture, stressing horizontality, which related the structure to the flat, Midwestern landscape, and creating an interrelationship between the interior and exterior of the house. The open-plan interiors were furnished with Wright's own designs, many of which were built-in to highlight the flow of the rooms. In 1936,

after a long period of inactivity during which his singular approach to architecture was out of step with the prevailing modern trends and the burgeoning International Style, Wright built the administrative headquarters for S. C. Johnson & Son in Racine, Wisconsin. This large office complex was one of the first in a series of buildings in which Wright used the curve as the predominant geometry. The form of the steel-and-wood workstations related to the interior design of the building and was Wright's elegant, spare interpretation of an American modern style.

RUSSEL WRIGHT
b. Lebanon, Ohio 1904–d. New York, New York 1976

Like Norman Bel Geddes and Henry Dreyfuss, Wright began his career in theater design, collaborating with Bel Geddes in 1924. By 1927 he began casting his papier-mâché theater props in metal, marketing them as household items. He then began to produce spun-aluminum objects such as pitchers and tea sets, which were so successful that he decided to open his own firm in 1930. Wright designed furniture for the Heywood-Wakefield Company, metal accessories for the Chase Brass and Copper Company, and household products, including his most famous work, the "American Modern" ceramic dinnerware, conceived in 1937 and produced between 1939 and 1957. His domestic items and furniture adapt the streamlined aesthetic to minimal, organic forms.

EVA ZEISEL
b. Budapest, Hungary 1906

Although Zeisel was trained as a painter, she was attracted to traditional Hungarian pottery and apprenticed to one of the few remaining folk potters. Her ceramics of the 1920s reflected Bauhaus and Deutscher Werkbund aesthetics of simple geometry and undecorated surfaces. She designed tableware, lamp bases, and inkwells, among other objects, for Schramberger Majolika Fabrik in Germany, and worked in the industrial production of ceramics in Leningrad and Moscow between 1932 and 1937. She was forced out of Russia in the Stalinist purges and returned to Hungary, from which she then fled the Nazis. In 1938 she arrived in New York via Vienna and England, where she met and married Hans Zeisel. Eva Zeisel taught at Pratt Institute in Brooklyn from 1939 to 1953. In her long career she designed china and tableware for Castleton China, Red Wing Potteries, Hall China, Sears Roebuck and Company, Rosenthal, and Noritake.

Glossary

ALUMINUM

Although available commercially since the turn of the century, aluminum did not become popular as a design material until the 1930s, when its physical properties—lightness, flexibility, resistance to corosion, and electrical conductivity—made it especially desirable to industrial designers. Aluminum was used for the streamlined bodies of racing cars, and an all-aluminum Pullman coach was displayed at the 1933 Chicago Century of Progress. It was also used for consumer goods, including utensils, stove-to-table ware, and furniture.

BAKELITE®

Bakelite is a synthetic resin formed by chemically combining phenols and formaldehydes. Although the inventor Dr. L. H. Baekland filed for the product's patent in 1907, commercial production did not begin until 1916. Bakelite is a durable, chemically resistant plastic that differs from other earlier plastics because it is thermosetting—it cannot be softened after it is heated. Furthermore, it is exceptionally useful as housing for electrical appliances because it does not conduct electricity. Its uses range from radio cabinets, telephone receivers, and electric insulators to elaborate costume jewelry and babies' teething rings.

CELLOPHANE

A thin, transparent, paperlike product made of viscose, cellophane was first patented in 1908 by a Swiss chemist, J. E. Brandemberger. With the help of his French-based firm La Cellophane, Brandemberger contracted with DuPont to manufacture the product by 1924. Cellophane is often used to wrap perishable goods because of its imperviousness to moisture and germs.

CELLULOID

Developed in 1869 by John Wesley Hyatt, celluloid is defined as the first synthetic plastic material. Made from a homogenous colloidal dispersion of cellulose nitrate and camphor, celluloid is a strong material resistant to water, oils, and diluted acids. While it was patented in 1871 as a material for dental plates, it was also used in hair combs, photographic films, and toys. Because of its flammability, safer synthetic polymers replaced it in the market. Despite this, it is still manufactured and used in Europe, Japan, and the United States.

DUCO

Invented in 1924 by DuPont, Duco is a lacquer that creates a shiny and quick-drying finishing surface. The product was a critical factor for the auto industry because it reduced the car-painting process from twenty-six days to only five hours, allowing assembly lines to manufacture cars at greater speed.

DULUX

A synthetic resin enamel invented in 1927 by DuPont, Dulux was, by 1930, used to improve the appearance of refrigerators.

FABRIKOID

A DuPont product used as a substitute for cloth and leather, fabrikoid is composed of a cloth foundation and a surface of collodion cotton, or pyroxylin.

FIBERGLASS

Fiberglass (or Fiberglas) is composed of glass that is spun into fibers by a stream of molten glass into a perforated spinning cup. One of its earliest uses included radar detection dishes during World War II, which were formed by mixing fiberglass with additional polymers. Shortly after the war, Charles Eames commissioned the Herman Miller Furniture Company to produce fiberglass shells for bucket-shaped seats.

FORMICA®

Formica is a surface material patented in 1922. Used to make laminated plastic products such as tabletops, wallboards, and furniture, it is created by impregnating special papers with synthetic resins, which are exposed to heat and pressure. Approximately seven sheets of paper are bonded together to make a surfacing material 1/16-inch thick. Its hard, smooth, surface can be colored and patterned in limitless varieties, and its finish can be dull or highly polished. Formica can withstand boiling water, heat, alcohol, and certain acids.

LUCITE®

Lucite is a DuPont product created during the 1930s. Also known as Plexiglas, it is composed of polymethyl methacrylate (a monomer), which is created when simple molecules of a flammable liquid known as ester methyl methacrylate are combined to form long chains (a polymer). This process, known as polymerization, can be caused by light and heat but is often produced through chemical catalysts. Lucite is quite stable and is resistant to shock and weathering. Although the material is transparent, it can be tinted by adding additional substances. It has many uses including boat windshields, aircraft windows, automobile lights, camera lenses, furniture, and decorative accessories. It is often used as a substitute for glass.

MONEL METAL

Monel Metal is a registered trademark of the International Nickel Company. Developed as early as 1905, Monel has been used in industrial projects as well as purely ornamental metalwork. Monel is made of alloys that contain nickel and copper in combination with iron, manganese, carbon, and silicon. It is often worked by casting and forging, although it can be used by cutting sheets into various shapes that are placed on top of one another to form interesting designs.

NYLON

Invented by DuPont in 1938, nylon is the first example of an entirely synthetic fiber. It is composed of rugged and flexible materials known as polymides. Because of its strength, luster, dyeability, and elasticity, nylon became a popular choice for use in apparel, upholstery, hosiery, lingerie, soft-sided luggage, carpeting, and even temperature-resistant packaging films.

RAYON

Rayon was developed as early as the nineteenth century as a substitute for silk. Interestingly, the material did not become popular until DuPont's introduction of the fiber in 1920. Rayon is formed when cellulose is treated with acetic acid and acetic anhydride, and then diffused. The substance is then extruded through a nozzle called a spinneret to form a fiber. It can be produced in long filaments but is usually cut into short lengths that are spun into yarn. The fiber shares similar characteristics with not only silk but also cotton. Because of this, it is often used in clothing apparel in various blends, and often where cotton would be incorporated. In addition, rayon can be used in automobile tires as well as in paper when mixed with wood pulp.

VITROLITE

A thick opaque structural glass manufactured by Libby-Owens-Ford, Vitrolite became especially popular in the years between the Great Depression and the outbreak of World War II. The product's versatility promoted various applications: it could be applied to both interior and exterior walls, as well as cut, laminated, sculpted, curved, colored, and textured. Today, it is most often used as an ornamental finish on surfaces exposed to the climate.

Notes

1. *Report of Commission Appointed by the Secretary of Commerce to Visit and Report upon the International Exposition of Modern Decorative and Industrial Art in Paris 1925,* 18–19.

2. Charles R. Richards, *Art in Industry* (New York: The Macmillan Company, 1929), 2.

3. Helen Appleton Read, "The Exposition in Paris: Part II," *International Studio* 82, no. 343 (Dec. 1925): 160.

4. Richards, 474.

5. The full story of The Metropolitan Museum of Art's role in promoting design in the twentieth century may be found in R. Craig Miller, *Modern Design, 1890–1990* (New York: The Metropolitan Museum of Art and Harry N. Abrams, Inc., 1990).

6. Richard F. Bach, *Bulletin of The Metropolitan Museum of Art* (Feb. 1923), 34.

7. There had been museum exhibitions of avant-garde design in the past, such as The Newark Museum's 1913 showing of modern German design; and in 1922 Joseph Urban opened a showroom of the Wiener Werkstätte in New York, but these were isolated instances and did not have any broad or lasting effect.

8. Herbert Lippman, "The Machine-Age Exhibition," *The Arts* 11, no. 6 (June 1927): 325.

9. Notes by Herman Rosse, transcribed by his daughter, Rosanne Rosse.

10. C. Adolph Glassgold, "The Decorative Arts," review in *The Arts* 14, no. 6 (Dec. 1928): 339–41.

11. Ibid.

12. Herman Rosse, writing in the catalogue of the exhibition.

13. Glassgold, "The Decorative Arts."

14. *Good Furniture Magazine* (June 1927): 277. The magazine began publication in 1913 as *Furniture Retailer and House Furnisher.* Between 1914 and June 1929 it was called *Good Furniture Magazine.* Its name was then changed to *Good Furniture and Decoration,* which it retained until September 1932, when the magazine lost its identity, being combined with *Interior Architecture and Decoration.*

15. Editorial, "Art Moderne Furniture Design in America; A Slowly Developing Vogue," *Good Furniture Magazine* (Oct. 1927): 190.

16. Ibid.

17. Editorial, "Modern Art in a Department Store: Wanamaker's Furnished Rooms Arouse Keen Interest," *Good Furniture Magazine* (Jan. 1928): 35.

18. Editorial, "Commercializing Art Moderne Furniture: Macy's Merchandising Plan Is Practical and Successful," *Good Furniture Magazine* (Jan. 1928): 30–31.

19. Editorial, "Art Moderne at the Midsummer Markets: The Outstanding Trend in Furniture," *Good Furniture Magazine* (Sept. 1928): 118.

20. Editorial, "Designers—European and American," *Good Furniture Magazine* (Apr. 1929): 167–68.

21. Schoen was in fact born in New York (see page 181). He protested the magazine's characterization of him as a foreigner and it subsequently printed a retraction.

22. Editorial, "Designers—European and American," 167–68.

23. Matlock Price, "Contempora," *Good Furniture Magazine* (Aug. 1929): 76.

24. Editorial, "Still a Question," *Good Furniture Magazine* (Sept. 1929): 7.

25. Editorial, "Where Are Our Moderns?" *Good Furniture Magazine* (Mar. 1930): n.p.

26. Editorial, "Out! The Millennium," *Good Furniture Magazine* (Apr. 1930): n.p.

27. Glassgold, "The Modern Note in Decorative Arts, Part Two," *The Arts* 13, no. 4 (Apr. 1928): 231.

28. Paul T. Frankl, "Just What Is This Modernistic Movement?" *Arts and Decoration* 29, no. 1 (May 1928): 57.

29. "Modernistic into Modern," *Arts and Decoration* 42, no. 1 (Nov. 1934): 12.

30. Frankl, "Just What Is This Modernistic Movement?" 108.

31. Ibid.

32. Jane Heap, "Machine Age Exposition," *The Little Review* 11, no. 1 (spring 1925): 23.

33. Ibid.

34. Aldous Huxley, *Creative Art* 7, no. 4 (Oct. 1930): 242.

35. William H. Baldwin, "Modern Art and the Machine Age," *The Independent* 119, no. 4023 (July 1927): 39.

36. For a full discussion of planned obsolescence, see Jeffrey L. Meikle, *Twentieth Century Limited* (Philadelphia: Temple University Press, 1991).

37. Bach, "Introduction," *The Architect and the Industrial Arts: An Exhibition of Contemporary Design* (New York: The Metropolitan Museum of Art, 1929), 24.

38. Henry W. Kent, "The Motive of the Exhibition of American Industrial Art," *Bulletin of The Metropolitan Museum of Art* 24, no. 4 (Apr. 1929): 97.

39. *The Architect and the Industrial Arts,* 45.

40. Ibid., 46.

41. The dressing table, designed by John H. Hopkins of Chicago, was later acquired by the Museum (1978.26.1).

42. Richards, "Exhibition of American Contemporary Design," *Bulletin of The Metropolitan Museum of Art* 24, no. 3 (Mar. 1929): 76.

43. Ibid.

44. "Modernistic into Modern," 12.

45. Richards, "A Present-day Outlook on Applied Art," *The Architectural Record* 77, no. 4 (Apr. 1935): 228–29.

46. Katharine Morrison Kahle, *Modern French Decoration* (New York: G. P. Putnam's Sons, 1930), 213.

47. Curtis Patterson, "A Source Book on Modern Interiors," *International Studio* 94 (Sept. 1929): 73.

48. Ralph Walker, "Contemporary American Industrial Art: 1940," *Bulletin of The Metropolitan Museum of Art* 35, no. 7 (July 1940): 140.

Bibliography

GENERAL

Adams, Maurice S. R. *Modern Decorative Art.* Philadelphia: J. B. Lippincott Company, 1930.

American Union of Decorative Artists and Craftsmen. *Annual of American Design 1931.* Robert L. Leonard and C. Adolph Glassgold, eds. New York: Ives Washburn, 1930.

_____. *Modern American Design.* Robert L. Leonard and C. Adolph Glassgold, eds. 1930. Reprint, New York: Acanthus Press, 1992.

Bush, Donald J. *The Streamlined Decade.* New York: George Braziller, 1975.

Byars, Mel. *The Design Encyclopedia.* London: Laurence King, 1994.

Cheney, Sheldon, and Martha Cheney. *Art and the Machine: An Account of Industrial Design in 20th-Century America.* New York: Whittlesey House, 1936.

Christ-Janer, Albert. *Eliel Saarinen.* Chicago: University of Chicago Press, 1948.

Dictionnaire Internationale des Arts Appliqués et du Design. Arlette Barré-Despond, ed. Paris: Éditions du Regard, 1996.

Dreyfuss, Henry. *Industrial Design: A Progress Report, 1929–1952.* New York: Davis, Delaney, n.d.

_____. *A Record of Industrial Design, 1929–1946.* New York: Davis, Delaney, n.d.

Du Pont: The Autobiography of an American Enterprise. New York: Charles Scribner's Sons, 1952.

Duncan, Alastair. *American Art Deco.* New York: Harry N. Abrams, 1986.

Dutton, William S. *Du Pont: One Hundred and Forty Years.* New York: Charles Scribner's Sons, 1942.

Encyclopedia of Interior Design. Joanna Banham, ed. 2 Vols. London: Fitzroy Dearborn Publishers, 1997.

Ferriss, Hugh. *The Metropolis of Tomorrow.* New York: Ives Washburn, 1929.

Ford, James, and Katherine Morrow Ford. *Design of Modern Interiors.* New York: Architectural Book Publishing Co., 1942.

Frankl, Paul T. *Form and Re-Form: A Practical Handbook of Modern Interiors.* New York: Harper and Brothers, 1930.

_____. *New Dimensions: The Decorative Arts of Today in Words and Pictures.* New York: Payson and Clarke, 1928.

_____. *Space for Living: Creative Interior Decoration and Design.* New York: Doubleday, Doren and Co., 1938.

Geddes, Norman Bel. *Horizons.* Boston: Little, Brown, and Company, 1932.

Greif, Martin. *Depression Modern: The Thirties Style in America.* New York: Universe Books, 1975.

Hanks, David A., with Jennifer Toher. *Donald Deskey: Decorative Designs and Interiors.* New York: E. P. Dutton, 1987.

Heinz, Thomas A. *Frank Lloyd Wright: Interiors and Furniture.* London: Academy Group, 1994.

Kahle, Katharine Morrison. *Modern French Decoration.* New York: G. P. Putnam's Sons, 1930.

Kahn, Ely Jacques. *Design in Art and Industry.* New York: Charles Scribner's Sons, 1935.

Kiesler, Frederick. *Contemporary Art Applied to the Store and Its Display.* New York: Brentano's, 1930.

Kostof, Spiro. *America by Design.* New York: Oxford University Press, 1987.

Landmarks of Twentieth-Century Design. Kathryn B. Hiesinger and George H. Marcus, eds. New York: Abbeville Press, 1993.

Loewy, Raymond. *Industrial Design.* Woodstock, NY: Overlook Press, 1979.

Marcus George H. *Functionalist Design: An Ongoing History.* Munich and New York: Prestel, 1995.

Meikle, Jeffrey L. *Twentieth Century Limited: Industrial Design in America, 1925–1939.* Philadelphia: Temple University Press, 1991.

Miller, R. Craig. *Modern Design in the Metropolitan Museum of Art 1890–1990.* New York: Metropolitan Museum of Art, 1990.

Official Guide Book of the Fair, 1933. Chicago: A Century of Progress, 1933.

Official Guide Book of the New York World's Fair, 1939. New York: Exposition Publications, 1939.

Park, Edwin Avery. *New Backgrounds for a New Age.* New York: Harcourt, Brace and Co., 1927.

Pulos, Arthur J. *American Design Ethic: A History of Industrial Design to 1940.* Cambridge: MIT Press, 1983.

Remington, R. Roger. *Lester Beall: Trailblazer of American Graphic Design.* New York: W. W. Norton and Co., 1996.

Richards, Charles R. *Art in Industry.* New York: W. E. Rudge, 1922.

_____. *Industrial Art and the Museum.* New York: Macmillan, 1927.

Rosenthal, Rudolph, and Helena L. Ratzka. *The Story of Modern Applied Art.* New York: Harper, 1948.

Sironen, Martha K. *A History of American Furniture.* East Stroudsburg, PA: Towse Publishing Co., 1936.

Sparke, Penny. *A Century of Design: Design Pioneers of the Twentieth Century.* Hauppauge, NY: Barron's, 1998.

Teague, Walter Dorwin. *Design This Day: The Technique of Order in the Machine Age.* New York: Harcourt, Brace and Co., 1940.

Van Doren, Harold. *Industrial Design: A Practical Guide.* New York: McGraw-Hill, 1940.

Wilson, Jack D. *Phoenix and Consolidated Art Glass 1926–1980.* Marietta, OH: Antique Publications, 1989.

Wittkopp, Gregory, ed. *Saarinen House and Garden: A Total Work of Art.* New York: Harry N. Abrams, 1995.

EXHIBITION CATALOGUES

American Federation of Arts. *International Exhibition of Ceramic Art.* The Metropolitan Museum of Art. New York, 1928.

_____. *International Exhibition of Glass and Rugs.* The Metropolitan Museum of Art. New York, 1929.

_____. *International Exhibition of Metalwork and Cotton Textiles.* Museum of Fine Arts. Boston, 1930.

American Industrial Art: Ninth Annual Exhibition of Current Manufactures Designed and Made in the United States. The Metropolitan Museum of Art. New York, 1925.

American Industrial Art: Tenth Annual Exhibition of Current Manufactures Designed and Made in the United States. The Metropolitan Museum of Art. New York, 1926.

The Architect and the Industrial Arts: An Exhibition of Contemporary American Design. The Metropolitan Museum of Art. New York, 1929.

Art Deco. Minneapolis Institute of Arts. Minneapolis, 1971.

Art in Industry in Buffalo. Buffalo Fine Arts Academy and Albright Art Gallery. Buffalo, 1932.

The Catalogue of the Exposition of Art in Trade at Macy's. R. H. Macy and Company. New York, 1927.

A Century of Design: Insights Outlook on a Museum of Tomorrow. Florian Hufnagl, ed. State Museum of Applied Arts. Munich, 1996.

Contempora Exposition of Art and Industry. Contempora, Inc. New York: 1929.

Contemporary American Industrial Art: Fifteenth Exhibition. The Metropolitan Museum of Art. New York, 1940.

Contemporary American Industrial Art: Thirteenth Exhibition. The Metropolitan Museum of Art. New York, 1934.

Davies, Karen. *At Home in Manhattan: Modern Decorative Arts, 1925 to the Depression*. Yale University Art Gallery. New Haven, CT, 1983.

Design for the Machine. Pennsylvania Museum. Philadelphia, 1932.

Design in America: The Cranbrook Vision, 1925–1950. Harry N. Abrams, Inc., in association with the Detroit Institute of Art and The Metropolitan Museum of Art, 1983.

Design 1935–1965: What Modern Was. Martin Eidelberg, ed. Musée des Arts Décoratifs du Montréal. Montreal, 1991.

Designing Modernity: The Arts of Reform and Persuasion, 1885–1945. Edited by Wendy Kaplan. The Wolfsonian. Miami Beach, FL, 1995.

Exposition Internationale des Arts Décoratifs et Industriels Modernes, 1925. 12 Vols. Paris: Larousse, 1928.

An Exposition of Modern French Decorative Art. Lord & Taylor. New York, 1928.

Fillin-Yeh, Susan. *Charles Sheeler: American Interiors*. Yale University Art Gallery. New Haven, CT, 1987.

Frederick Carder: His Life and Work. Corning Museum of Glass. Corning, NY, 1952.

Gardner, Paul. V. *Frederick Carder: Portrait of a Glassmaker*. Corning Museum of Glass. Corning, NY, 1985.

Gebhard, David, and Harriet von Brenton. *Kem Weber: The Moderne in Southern California*. Art Galleries, University of California. Santa Barbara, CA, 1969.

Hennessey, William J. *Russel Wright: American Designer*. Gallery Association of New York State. Hamilton, NY, 1983.

High Styles: Twentieth-Century American Design. Whitney Museum of American Art. New York, 1985.

International Exposition of Art in Industry. R. H. Macy and Company. New York, 1928.

Johnson, Philip. *Machine Art*. Museum of Modern Art. New York, 1934.

Machine-Age Exposition. The Little Review 12, no. 1, supplement (May 1927).

The 1920s: Age of the Metropolis. Jean Clair, ed. Montreal Museum of Fine Arts. Montreal, 1991.

Raymond Loewy: Pioneer of American Industrial Design. International Design Center. Berlin, 1990.

Rugs and Carpets: An International Exhibition of Contemporary Industrial Art. The Metropolitan Museum of Art. New York, 1937.

Tenth Exhibition of Contemporary American Industrial Art. The Metropolitan Museum of Art. New York, 1931.

Visions of Tomorrow: New York and American Industrialization in the 1920s–1930s. Isetan Museum of Art. Tokyo, 1988.

William Lescaze. Institute for Architecture and Urban Studies. New York, 1982.

Wilson, Richard Guy, Dianne H. Pilgrim, and Dickran Tashjian. *The Machine Age in America, 1918–1941*. Brooklyn Museum of Art. Brooklyn, 1986.

PERIODICALS

Advertising & Selling (vols. 16–24, 1930–35).

Advertising Arts (no volume numbers, 1930–35); supplement to *Advertising & Selling*.

American Architect (vols. 127–48, 1925–36); continued as *American Architect and Architecture* (vols. 148–52, 1936–38).

American Magazine of Art (vols. 16–29, 1925–36); continued as *Magazine of Art* (vols. 30–34, 1937–41).

Architectural Forum (vols. 42–75, 1925–41).

Architectural Record (vols. 57–90, 1925–41).

Architecture (vols. 51–73, 1925–36).

Art et Décoration (vols. 48–67, 1925–38; new series, no. 1, 1938; ceased publication 1939–45).

The Arts (vols. 7–18, 1925–31); absorbed by *Arts Weekly* (vol. 1, 1932).

Arts & Decoration (vols. 22–54, 1925–41).

Atelier (vols. 1–2, 1931); continued as *London Studio* (vols. 3–17, 1932–39).

California Arts & Architecture (vols. 40–61, 1929–41).

Commercial Art (vols. 4–5, 1925–26; new series, vols. 1–11, 1926–31); continued as *Commercial Art and Industry* (vols. 12–20, 1932–36); continued as *Art and Industry* (vols. 21–31, 1936–41).

Creative Art (vols. 1–12, 1927–33); absorbed by *American Magazine of Art* (vols. 27–29, 1934–36).

Decorators Digest (vols. 1–7, 1932–36); continued as *Interior Design and Decoration* (vols. 8–18, 1937–42).

Design (vols. 26–43, 1925–41).

Good Furniture Magazine (vols. 24–32, 1925–29); continued as *Good Furniture & Decoration* (vols. 33–37, 1929–31);

combined with *Interior Architecture & Decoration* (vols. 37–38, 1931–32).

House & Garden (vols. 47–80, 1925–41).

Industrial Arts Magazine (vols. 14–19, 1925–30); continued as *Industrial Arts and Vocational Education* (vols. 20–30, 1930–41).

Industrial Education Magazine (vols. 26–41, 1925–39).

Interior Architecture & Decoration (vols. 1–2, 1931); combined with *Good Furniture & Decoration* (vols. 37–38, 1931–32).

International Studio (vols. 80–99, 1925–31); absorbed by *The Connoisseur* (vols. 88–108, 1931–41).

The Little Review (vols. 1–12, 1914–1926; final issue 1929).

Metal Arts (vols. 1–3, 1928–30); continued as *Metalcraft* (vols. 4–9, 1930–32).

Pencil Points (vols. 6–26, 1925–41).

Parnassus (vols. 1–13, 1929–41).

Upholsterer and Interior Decorator (vols. 74–94, 1925–35); continued as *Interior Decorator* (vols. 95–100, 1935–41).

ARTICLES

"American Modernist Furniture Inspired by Sky-Scraper Architecture." *Good Furniture Magazine* 29, no. 3 (September 1927): 119–21.

Anderson, Harry V. "Contemporary American Designers: George Sakier." *Decorators Digest* 5, no. 1 (July 1935): 38–41.

_____. "Contemporary American Designers: Ilonka Karasz." *Decorators Digest* 5, no. 6 (December 1935): 46–49, 87.

_____. "Contemporary American Designers: Lurelle Guild." *Decorators Digest* 4, no. 2 (February 1935): 42, 82, 84.

_____. "Ruth Reeves." *Design* 37, no. 9 (March 1936): 24–26, 39.

"The Architect and the Industrial Arts: An Exhibition of Contemporary American Design, Metropolitan Museum of Art." *American Magazine of Art* 20, no. 4 (April 1929): 201–12.

Arens, Egmont. "Next Year's Cars." *American Magazine of Art* 29, no. 11 (November 1936): 730–36.

"Art and Machines: Examples of the Art of and for the Machine as Shown in Two New York Exhibitions." *Architectural Forum* 60, no. 5 (May 1934): 331–35.

Bauer, Catherine. "'Machine-Made.'" *American Magazine of Art* 27, no. 5 (May 1934): 267–70.

"Beauty of Form in Machine Art." *Design* 35, no. 10 (April 1934): 8–9, 25–26.

Bonney, Louise. "Modern Fabrics." *Atelier* 1 (June 1931): 256–61.

"'A Century of Progress' in Art." *London Studio* 6 (October 1933): 191–93.

Clute, Eugene. "Craftsmanship in Decorated Glass." *Architecture*

64, no. 1 (July 1931): 11–16.

"Contemporary American Industrial Art." *American Magazine of Art* 24, no. 4 (April 1932): 274–76.

"Contemporary American Industrial Design." *Architectural Record* 87, no. 6 (June 1940): 88–91.

Dana, John Cotton. "American Applied Art and the Department Store." *Newark Museum* 2, no. 6 (March 1929): 42–43.

_____. "Is the Department Store a Museum?" *Newark Museum* 2, no. 1 (July–August 1928): 1–2.

"Designers for Mass Production: Lurelle Guild develops mechanical improvement as well as eye-appeal." *Art and Industry* 24, no. 144 (June 1938): 228–33.

"Exhibit of American Designers' Gallery: An Ambitious Program in Art Moderne." *Good Furniture Magazine* 32, no. 1 (January 1929): 40–45.

"Fabrics—Primitives and Sophisticates." *Arts & Decoration* 42, no. 5 (March 1935): 8–10.

Fawcett, Waldon. "The Future of the Art-in-Trade Exposition." *Good Furniture Magazine* 31, no. 5 (November 1928): 285–86.

"Features of the American Designers' Gallery Exhibition." *Metal Arts* 1, no. 2 (December 1928): 81–84, 119.

Frankl, Paul T. "Furniture of the Fourth Dimension Designed for the New Interior." *House & Garden* 51, no. 2 (February 1927): 76–77, 140.

_____. "Modern Will Live." *California Arts & Architecture* 53, no. 3 (March 1938): 16–19.

Frankl, Paul T., and Henry F. Bultitude. "Furniture for the House of Tomorrow." *Architecture* 69, no. 4 (April 1934): 189–96.

"Gilbert Rohde Suggests a Plan for Built-In Furniture." *London Studio* 13, no. 72 (March 1937): 150–56.

Glassgold, C. Adolph. "Decorative Art Notes." *The Arts* 13, no. 5 (May 1928): 296–301.

_____. "The Decorative Arts." *The Arts* 14, no. 6 (October 1928): 214–17.

_____. "Modern American Industrial Design." *Arts & Decoration* 35, no. 3 (July 1931): 30–31, 87.

_____. "The Modern Note in Decorative Arts." Parts 1 and 2. *The Arts* 13, nos. 3–4 (March–April 1928): 153–67, 221–35.

Gorham, I. B. "Comfort Convenience Colour: Examples from the Designs of Kem Weber on the Pacific Coast." *Creative Art* 7, no. 4 (October 1930): 248–53.

Green, Kneeland L. "Modern Life, Ordinary Things, Design: Americana Fabrics." *Creative Art* 4, no. 2 (February 1929): 102–07.

Hanks, David A., and Jennifer Toher. "Donald Deskey's Decorative Designs." *The Magazine Antiques* 131, no. 4 (April 1987): 838–45.

Haskell, Douglas. "Cheaper, Better Homes." *Creative Art* 4, no. 5 (May 1929): xl–xli.

Heaton, Maurice. "I Am a Craftsman." *Architectural Forum* 70, no. 3 (March 1939): 204.

"Henry Dreyfuss Designs New 'Century' Train." *Design* 40, no. 7 (February 1939): 5–7.

Hitchcock, Henry-Russell, Jr. "Some American Interiors in the Modern Style." *Architectural Record* 64, no. 3 (September 1928): 235–43.

Komanecky, Michael. "The Screens and Screen Designs of Donald Deskey." *The Magazine Antiques* 131, no. 5 (May 1987): 1064–77.

McGregor, Donald. "AUDAC in Brooklyn: A Great Museum Host to Moderns." *Good Furniture & Decoration* 36, no. 6 (June 1931): 322–25.

"Machine Art." *Art Digest* 6, no. 10 (15 February 1932): 15.

"Machine Art." *Commercial Art and Industry* 16, no. 95 (May 1934): 177–82.

"Metal in the Metropolitan Museum Exhibition." *Metal Arts* 2, no. 2 (February 1929): 107–12.

"Metals in Interior Decoration." *Metal Arts* 1, no. 1 (November 1928): 38–46.

"Metropolitan Contemporary Industrial Art Exhibit Opens." *Metal Arts* 7, no. 4 (October 1931): 144–45.

Migennes, Pierre. "Un Artiste décorateur américain Paul Th. Frankl." *Art et décoration* 53 (January–June 1928): 49–56.

_____. "Ombres portées et décor de tissus." *Art et décoration* 51 (January–June 1927): 140–42.

Müller-Munk, Peter. "Industrial Design." *Design* 38, no. 7 (January 1937): 12–15.

_____. "Machine—Hand." *Creative Art* 5, no. 4 (October 1929): 709–12.

"A New Century of Progress." *Design* 35, no. 10 (April 1934): 10, 24.

Ostergard, Derek, and David A. Hanks. "Gilbert Rohde and the Evolution of Modern Design, 1927–1941." *Arts Magazine* 56, no. 2 (October 1981): 98–107.

"Plumbing by Mr. Sakier." *Arts & Decoration* 42, no. 5 (March 1935): 42–43.

Reid, Kenneth. "Masters of Design 2—Norman Bel Geddes." *Pencil Points* 18, no. 1 (January 1937): 1–32.

Rohde, Gilbert. "Aptitudes and Training for Industrial Design." *Parnassus* 13, no. 2 (February 1941): 60–64.

_____. "The Design Laboratory." *American Magazine of Art* 29, no. 10 (October 1936): 638–43, 686.

_____. "What Is Industrial Design?" *Design* 38, no. 6 (December 1936): 3–5.

Sanford, N. C. "An International Exhibit of Modern Art: Macy's of New York Sponsored Forward-Looking Event." *Good Furniture Magazine* 31, no. 1 (July 1928): 15–20.

Schoen, Eugene. "Design in Materials." *Architecture* 73, no. 2 (February 1936): 119–22.

_____. "The Design of Modern Interiors." *Creative Art* 2, no. 5 (May 1928): xl–xliii.

_____. "House & Garden's Modern Home." *House & Garden* 55, no. 2 (February 1929): 94–95.

_____. "Industrial Design: A New Profession." *Magazine of Art* 31, no. 8 (August 1938): 472–79.

Schwartz, Jane. "Exhibition of Machine Art Now on View at Modern Museum." *Art News* 32, no. 23 (10 March 1934): 4.

"Steuben Glass." *London Studio* 9, no. 49 (April 1935): 206–09.

Storey, Walter Rendell. "The Roots of Modern Design." *Design* 37, no. 9 (March 1936): 3–7, 38.

Susswein, Rita. "The AUDAC Exhibition at the Brooklyn Museum." *Parnassus* 3, no. 5 (May 1931): 14–15.

Van Doren, Harold. "Designing for Appearance." *Design* 37, no. 9 (March 1936): 10–21, 39.

_____. "Industrial Design and the Manufacturer." *Design* 38, no. 2 (June 1936): 20–23, 44.

Vogelgesang, Shepard. "Contemporary Interior Design Advances." *Good Furniture Magazine* 32, no. 5 (May 1929): 229–34.

Weber, Kem. "Bit by Bit." *California Arts & Architecture* 57, no. 6 (June–July 1940): 22–23.

Young, Stark. "Decorative Textiles by Ruth Reeves." *American Magazine of Art* 22, no. 1 (January 1931): 31–33.

American Federation of Arts

Mr. and Mrs. Peter Hobart
Mr. and Mrs. Eric Hoffman
Mr. and Mrs. H. Earl Hoover
Mrs. R.D. Hubbard
Arlyn Imberman
Mr. and Mrs. Warren Kanders
William W. Karatz
Elaine P. Kend
Nanette Laitman
Mr. and Mrs. Anthony M. Lamport
Natalie Ann Lansburgh
Mrs. Richard Livingston
Mr. and Mrs. Jeffrey M. Loewy
Mr. and Mrs. Lester B. Loo
Mrs. Mark O. L. Lynton
Mr. and Mrs. Angus MacDonald
Mr. and Mrs. Cargill MacMillan, Jr.
Mr. and Mrs. Richard Manoogian
Mr. and Mrs. Jeffrey Marcus
Luella Maslon
Mr. and Mrs. Robert Menschel
Mr. and Mrs. Eugene Mercy, Jr.
Marlene Meyerson
Mary S. Myers
Mrs. Peter Roussel Norman
Mr. and Mrs. George P. O'Leary
Mr. and Mrs. William Osterman
Patricia M. Patterson
Selma Pearl
Elizabeth Petrie
Mrs. Nicholas R. Petry
Mrs. Edward M. Pinsof
Mr. and Mrs. John W. Pitts
Mr. and Mrs. Harvey R. Plonsker
Mr. and Mrs. Lawrence S. Pollock, Jr.

Mr. and Mrs. Robert Pond
Howard E. Rachofsky
Mr. and Mrs. Edward Redstone
Mr. and Mrs. D.S. Reid
Edward R. Roberts
Mr. and Mrs. Jonathan P. Rosen
Mrs. Richard L. Rosenthal
Felice T. Ross
Mr. and Mrs. Lawrence Ruben
Mr. and Mrs. Samuel Rubinstein
Marc Sander
Helen H. Scheidt
Mr. and Mrs. Paul C. Schorr, III
Mr. Lowell M. Schulman and
    Ms. Dianne Wallace
Adriana Seviroli
Mr. and Mrs. Eric P. Sheinberg
Mr. and Mrs. Michael Sheldon
Mr. and Mrs. Matthew R. Simmons
Mrs. Dory Small
Janet R. Stern
Mrs. James G. Stevens
Mr. and Mrs. Harry F. Stimpson, Jr.
Ms. Linda M. Swartz
Mrs. Richard Swig
Mr. and Mrs. Jeff Tarr
Rosalie Taubman
Mr. and Mrs. Harry Tenenbaum
Mr. and Mrs. William B. Troy
Alice S. Warren
Mrs. Robert C. Warren
Mr. and Mrs. Alan Weeden
Mrs. Richard Weil
Mr. and Mrs. Guy A. Weill
Mr. and Mrs. T. Evans Wyckoff

BENEFACTORS CIRCLE

Mr. and Mrs. Steven Ames
Mr. and Mrs. Glenn W. Bailey
Mr. and Mrs. Frank B. Bennett
Ruth Bowman
Mr. and Mrs. James Brice
Melva Bucksbaum
Iris Cantor
Mr. and Mrs. Donald M. Cox
Mr. David L. Davies and
    Mr. John D. Weeden
Mr. and Mrs. Kenneth N. Dayton
Mr. and Mrs. C. Douglas Dillon
Mr. and Mrs. William Etheridge
Mrs. Donald Findlay
Mr. and Mrs. John A. Friede
Mrs. Melville W. Hall
Mr. and Mrs. Lee Hills
Mr. and Mrs. Theodore S. Hochstim
Mr. and Mrs. Gilbert H. Kinney
Mr. and Mrs. Richard S. Lane
Mr. and Mrs. Robert E. Linton
Mr. and Mrs. Henry Luce III
Jeanne Lang Mathews
Mr. and Mrs. Frederick R. Mayer
Mrs. C. Blake McDowell, Jr.
Mr. and Mrs. Robert M. Meltzer
Mr. Robert M. Meltzer
Mr. and Mrs. Nicholas Millhouse
Mrs. Nancy B. Negley
Roy R. Neuberger
Honorable and Mrs. Leon B. Polsky
Mr. and Mrs. Milton F. Rosenthal
Barbara Slifka

Mr. and Mrs. Michael R. Sonnenreich
Ann C. Stephens
Mr. and Mrs. John W. Straus
Mr. and Mrs. David J. Supino
Virginia Ullman
Mr. and Mrs. Michael J. Waldman
Mr. and Mrs. Martin S. Weinberg
Mr. and Mrs. Herbert Wittow

Index

191

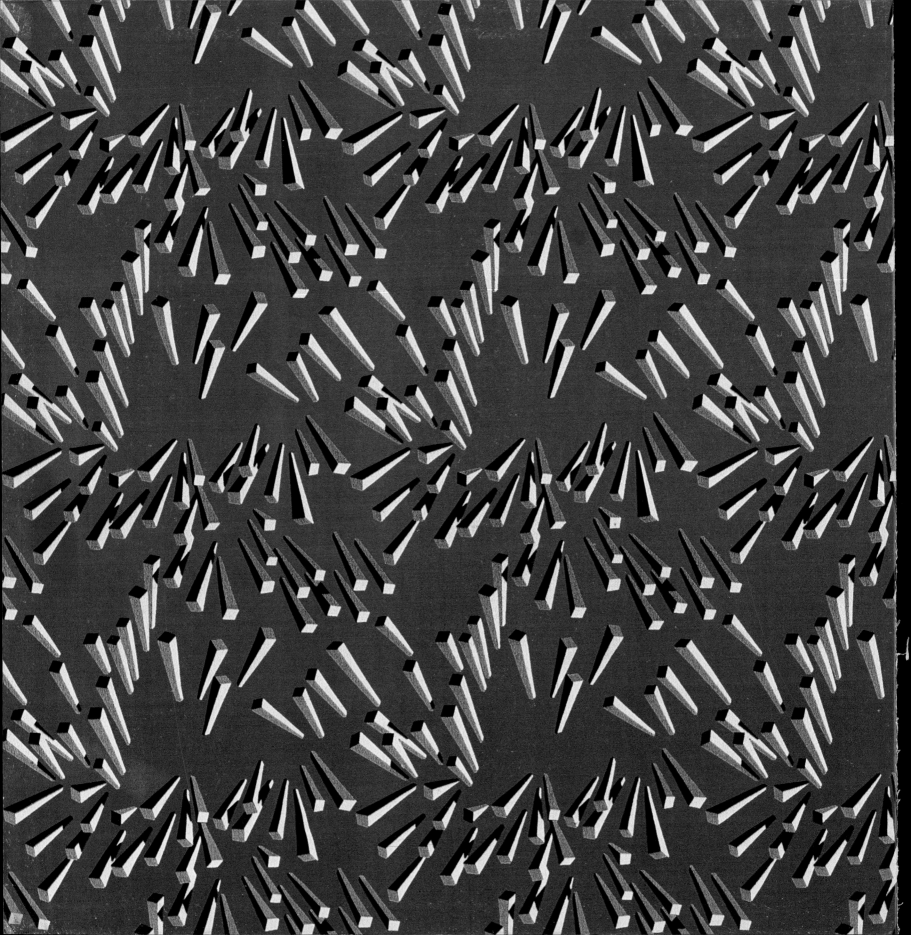